A socially irresponsible, economically distorted, and politically incorrect parable with

BIG NUTS

by Neil Barry

Summary

In the Boardroom of Dough Inc., the #1 manufacturer of donuts, éclairs, and sundry fattening pastries, the executive team grapples with the company's future. Little do they know, the State Governor, his trusty campaign advisor, and his aide de camp, are meeting with a concerned pediatric oncologist, self-appointed head of her newly formed Healthy Children Action Committee. Together, they plan a new government-led assault to save weight-challenged kids from high calorie foods. Worse, Dough Inc.'s major competitor is launching Big Nuts, donuts with 784 calories.

Dough Inc. responds to both challenges with imitation, outsourcing, automation, bribery, and outright theft. Only Jeremy McTavish, head of New Product Development, has a solution.

Author's note: I could tell you more about what happens with Big Nuts, but then you might not read the rest of the book. That would be unfortunate. When you read it, you'll laugh your ass off. However, don't blame me when it hurts to sit down; you chose to keep reading.

In Appreciation

The author extends his heartfelt appreciation to those shameless, courageous, anonymous people who dared to support him in writing BIG NUTS, and bringing it to public attention. In particular, the author offers his insincere gratitude to the mass media, corruptors of minds, and politicians who infuriated him so much with miss-speaking (aka lies), mistruths (aka bigger lies), and brazen omissions of fact, that he had no alternative but to write and publish this timely ~~parable~~ parody.

For slightly more serious Neil Barry books, visit his website: neilbarrybooks.com

Contents

Chapter 1.

"The future is now! Being the best that we can be! Building on strengths! Overcoming diversity! Survival of the fittest is why we're here," Herman Stiche II boomed. "Strategic planning, from goals and objectives all the way down to doing whatever it takes to make more out of Dough!"

Having delivered his inspiring introductory remarks, he imposed himself before the presidents' portraits and staunchly surveyed his executive team. Behind him, on his right, his bellicose great grandfather, Herman Stiche I, gazed with grim determination through a gilded frame. On his left side, his grandfather, Marvin, also of weighty substance, sternly regarded those gathered for the weekly management meeting in the Dough Inc. Boardroom.

Herman (the second) shared more than a name with his great grandfather. Both men filled a room; however, Herman (the first) looked sporty in yachting attire. He'd stood for his portrait, his left hand raised to his forehead as if scanning the horizon like Captain Ahab on the lookout for a great white whale. His blotchy right hand grasped a Cuban cigar as big as a cinnamon stick, not the one that eventually choked him. However, instead of developing the maritime theme, the artist had posthumously painted the portly president in the very same boardroom. He took the liberty of adding a fireplace, its ornate mantel bearing a silver tea service and an English-china rose-pattern platter with two sprinkled, strawberry-iced donuts, and a symbolic cinnamon stick.

As the plump ten-year-old heir to the Stiche fortune, Herman II had learned clothes were as important as character. However, stance also defined the man. With this in mind, he lodged his left hand like a corporate Napoleon in the pocket of his made-to-order blazer, navy-blue with gold anchor buttons. It made him feel like a ship's captain, in complete control of his vessel. His crew looked back with attentive gaze. He squared his shoulders and elevated his chin, stretching a flabby roll from his neck before he charged on.

"Let's do it, y'all! We'll start off with a swot!"

His practiced voice of authority should have commanded attention; cross-eyed, he just looked bewildered.

"Swat," Ms. Wick squeaked, transcribing rapidly in squiggly shorthand.

Ms. Wick was a spinster, born and bred in Sevierville, Tennessee, a few miles down the road from the mystical mecca of Gatlinburg. It was her responsibility as Mr. Stiche's personal secretary to promptly issue no more than two pages of typed and spell-checked minutes for every executive meeting, which she took to mean transcribing every one of Stiche's pearls of wisdom. Suddenly, her head snapped up, steel-grey eyes blazing, her careful coiffeur of silver-blond coils bouncing like Dolly Parton at the height of a love song.

"Should I cover the goodies?" she asked, searching for a fly on the platter of donuts.

She'd personally selected donuts from the production line and stacked them five high on the now-chipped English-china rose-pattern platter. She offset each layer to minimize contact, sticky and easily squashed cream-filled donuts on top, more substantial cake donuts on the bottom, and in between plain, sugared, and Ms. Wick's personal favorite, honey-iced hazelnut.

As if her ears picked up a distant buzz, she unexpectedly directed her frown from the donut-cornucopia in the center of the table to the French doors. The French doors were a likely entrance for invading species; however, they were locked tight in early March. It might have been too cold for flies, yet she still scrutinized

2

the opposite wall, hoping to spot the loathsome intruder among the Stiche family portraits.

Her gaze passed over each Stiche framed in gold; treasured masterpieces of the company's presidents on dark mahogany paneling. She began with dour Friedrich, company founder and inventor of the sticky Stiche Bun. He was brilliantly businesslike despite a mediocre gene pool. He was not someone who a girl took home to meet mother; although he'd finally married a young freckled lady from Wichita. Their only offspring was hapless Herman (the first). It was Herman, just back from a jaunt in sunny Havana, who'd watched the factory burn to the ground two days after he'd cancelled the insurance policy to save money during the Great Depression. Boldly; some would say foolishly; he borrowed vast sums of money to rebuild, taking advantage of starvation wages to construct a monument to the snack food industry.

The Stiche Building—still the company's headquarters; had a first floor built from the finest Indiana limestone, creamy-white like bread dough, with five lesser floors of yellowish sandstone rising above. Herman's neoclassical edifice to enterprise was topped with a Mansard roof of dark brown, yellow, and red roof tiles. It was an architect's parody of a Stiche Bun, complete with chocolate icing and sprinkles.

"Is that a fly?" Ms. Wick inquired, putting down her stenographer's pad and flouncing up in a festive floral frock— spring was right around the corner in Sevierville's outlet malls, where she'd spent the last three weekends.

She went over to peer at a speck on Stanley Stiche. He was the eldest of Herman's ten overfed children, whose claim to fame was changing the company name from Stiche Bun Company to Dough Inc. just a week before he asphyxiated himself on a slice of Dutch apple pie. His portrait was also painted posthumously. He was posed imaginatively, holding a cherished chocolate donut in lieu of pie.

Stanley's brother, Marvin, took over the reins, starting the corporate wagon on a different trajectory. After Marvin came his eldest son, Douglas, who assumed the crown after attending Harvard University for two less-than-stellar years. He filed for bankruptcy three times before he choked on a wiener at the company picnic. Douglas' bereaved wife, Dorothea, demanded 'no donuts' for his portrait. The artist had added them anyway; a cup of tea and a cream-filled raspberry sitting on the artistic-license mantle. At the end of the line, there was Herman II, who hadn't choked on anything, yet. At first glance, the same artist might have painted all of them.

"It's a booger," Ms. Wick muttered, inaudibly blaming the janitor as she returned to her seat.

"Where was I?" Herman said, thinking festive floral, though colorful, wasn't conducive to corporate rigor. "Oh, yes, SWOT."

"I don't know why you'd need a fly swatter."

"SWOT, Ms. Wick. Not SWAT! It stands for strengths, weaknesses, opportunities, and threats!" Thomas G. Babcock had a ridiculous fake-Boston accent, made worse when he rounded his mouth to a thin-lipped oval to emphasize 'O.'

"Right you are, Tom! You're on the ball," Herman applauded. "No flies to be swatted today, Ms. Wick. Now, like I was sayin', the purpose of today's meeting is strategic planning."

"As if the best snack-food company in the free world needs to do strategic planning," Babcock chuckled, making a point of straightening his custom made-in-China tie. It featured circles in brown and white on creamy-hued silk, possibly chocolate and vanilla-iced donuts on grandma's lace doily.

Ms. Wick scowled down the Boardroom table at the overzealous Senior Vice President of Finance. As luck would have it, before she could mutter a word, Chairman Herman intervened.

"That's a good point, Tom. I know I don't need to tell you that a regular strategy session is good business practice. Make sure our corporate ship's headed in the right direction. Don't want to hit any icebergs, do we?"

"We have God at the helm, don't we Ms. Wick?" Babcock declared with a smarmy smirk.

For three weeks each year Ms. Wick lived on a Caribbean cruise ship; the rest of the time she lived for Jesus, the company, and visiting outlet malls. Her rose quartz earrings imitated strawberry donuts; recognition of her 35 years with Dough Inc. When she went to the supermarket, she wore the company T-shirt, bright red with two large vanilla-iced donuts in front and 'Dough Family Picnic' on her back.

While spinster and Senior VP glared at each other, Stiche stalked from past to present, from presidential portraits to a whiteboard on a rickety easel symbolically placed at the front of the room. In big black letters at the top, he wrote 'S,' space, 'W,' smaller space, 'O, 'much smaller space, and a very cramped 'T.'

"Strengths of the company?" he intoned. While he waited, he drew lines for four columns and underlined 'S'. Then, he stepped back. "Let's have them, y'all."

"Strawberry Puffs!"

"Right you are, Jeremy."

Jeremy McTavish puffed out his chest. Without a doubt, Strawberry Puffs were his finest achievement in the company. Puffs weren't technically donuts, if a donut required a hole in the center. Puffs were fried dough balls injected with strawberry jelly and a generous dollop of artificial, very sweet cream; but they weren't

5

like other jelly-filled donuts. The dough was spongier, almost lighter than air, the jelly was thicker (thanks to cornstarch), and the cream was fluffier (because of copious carbon dioxide infusion). They outsold the competition three to one, without a penny of advertising.

"Our commitment to the community is the best in the industry," Regina King said promptly.

She was a people-person, both VP of Personnel and Director of Public Relations. She dedicated herself to building lasting relationships. She took PR to new heights, communicating with anyone outside the company about Stiche superiority in the cake, pastry, and doughnut industry, warranted or not. She firmly believed that business success came from community involvement, whether providing donuts to the homeless, or sponsoring research into diabetes.

"So is our commitment to quality." Leo Frank was VP of quality control, 'Mr. QC,' outside the Boardroom.

"Not so fast, y'all. I need to get them down," Stiche complained, trying to fit 'Strawberry puffs' on one line.

"Herman, underneath quality control you should put highest quality ingredients, manufacturing to exacting standards, and timely distribution. Quality is numero uno in all our operations," Leo extolled. "Cut the quality and people stop buying."

"I can't write all that. You'll need to summarize," Stiche grumped, running into the 'W' column with 'puffs.'

"It's capital 'P' for Puffs," someone pointed out.

No one ever questioned Herman II was a direct descendent of Friedrich Stiche; they shared a receding hairline, bulging jowls, bushy eyebrows, and a big veiny nose. Nonetheless, Friedrich was imposing in his cleverly posed head-and-shoulders portrait. Like the sole Stiche bun on the rose-patterned platter in the foreground, Friedrich also seemed lonely, although he possessed presence in abundance, partly personality, mostly paunch. Like choking, size ran in the family, and Herman II was the biggest of five Stiche generations. He nudged 305 pounds in tight XXXL boxers. His shirt, executive blue with a button-down starched collar, had a 24-inch neck.

"How's this for a summary, Herman? We have a 32.3 percent market share and sales of $432 million a year. Our profit margin is the highest in the industry. We're number one, thanks to you, Herman," Babcock declared, mentally preparing for challenges from Regina and Leo.

"Only because of quality control!"

"And community involvement!"

"Just icing on the donut. I was going to add that our success is because of leadership at the top." Babcock stared them down simultaneously.

"Thank you, Tom, but it's really great people making a high quality product at a reasonable price," Stiche intervened. "All strengths that give us a competitive advantage."

He wrote 'people,' 'poduct,' and 'price' under 'S.'

Herman's portrait was the end of the line, since Herman was still without issue. It was just before the door to his office. He'd gone to his portrait-sitting in checkered trousers and a grass-green golfing jacket, hoping to appear audacious like his sea-faring great-grandfather. His grandfather, Marvin, was dull by comparison, yet he was the Stiche recognized as the captain of industry. Someone at Harvard Business School wrote a book about Marvin because of the company's contribution to the war effort— Dough Inc. thrived, selling red-white-and-blue 'Eat Uncle Sam' donuts to factory workers.

Corpulent Marvin squeezed into austere khaki for his portrait, a Douglas MacArthur-style suit with oversized epaulets. With his pale complexion and seated in a frumpy Victorian chair with a four-color map of the world on the wall behind him, Marvin resembled a stuffed army general, an impression confirmed by a mess hall tray full of patriotic donuts beside him—he died from plain overeating. He was so inspired by Dugout Doug's Pacific maneuvers that he smoked a corncob pipe and named his son Douglas Arthur.

Douglas Arthur was equally pretentious. Herman II's pasty-faced father was painted in a puce sweater with a Harvard crimson coat of arms. Douglas looked academically distinguished, holding a leather-bound *A Beginner's Guide to Ethics in American Business*. He'd personally selected a chocolate éclair, a Dough Inc. stalwart underestimated by donut lovers everywhere.

"We'll come back to strengths," Stiche decided, looking around. "Weaknesses? Anyone?"

"Do we have any worth mentioning?" Babcock swiftly replied.

"Every company has weaknesses, Tom. We don't make a perfect product."

Leo's head snapped around. "Not true, Regina. We don't tolerate imperfection in my department. If it isn't the best, it goes in the trash, not out the door."

"I don't know about that. Most of our equipment is out of date, Mr. Stiche. All of our fryers should be replaced, and the icing machines. We're lucky if half of them work at the same time. We ought to upgrade to the 500 series."

Everyone looked at Max Nussbaum. Six months from retiring, and always complaining, he looked like he was ready to doze off. He started with Stiche Bun Company the same day he

8

finished high school. From a summer job lugging bags of sugar from the loading dock to the hoppers in the basement, he worked his way up to the second floor fryers. After learning how to operate icing machines and cream injectors, he advanced to sugar-coaters on the third floor, while taking night classes in engineering. By the time he was junior assistant to the production manager, he'd disassembled every machine down to its last nut and bolt, including all 26 mixers—he was small enough to climb inside and replace agitators.

"We ought to do a lot of things," Babcock said under his breath, his granite gaze fixed on Nussbaum.

"We'll get to them with opportunities." Stiche underlined 'o' three times to keep the discussion on track.

He'd asked the artist to soften his blotchy pallor, and he'd been pleased when he saw the end result on canvas. Forgiving pastel tones and fuzzy brush strokes made him look like a divinely inspired golfer, one who was marginally overweight, not morbidly obese. Unfortunately, the artist had been less generous with the gleam of halogen light on the polished dome of his balding head; and the Strawberry Puff that Ms. Wick had artfully arranged with her favorite teacup and saucer looked stale. At the end of the day, his portrait didn't measure up to his father's.

"Weaknesses, y'all?" he asked in dead silence, his morning powdered-cappuccino coffee souring to acid reflux.

"Marketing is our biggest weakness, Herman, followed by NPD," Babcock said, shooting a glance down the table.

"NPD," Ms. Wick repeated, pencil at the ready. "Stands for..." She looked up hopefully.

"New Product Development," Babcock snapped. He'd recommended renaming Jeremy's Research & Development Group.

A surprised Herman II looked away from the whiteboard. "Did I hear you say Jeremy's area is a weakness?"

Babcock also recommended having NPD report to him, rather than directly to Herman.

"Herman, we need to focus new product development on ventures with a high likelihood of profitability."

He wasn't squeamish about discussing weaknesses, marketing, NPD, or anything else. Toes were made to be stepped on, the harder the better; spare the executive's self-esteem, spoil the company's reputation; a fourth Dough Inc. bankruptcy right around the corner if he let up the pressure.

"Next week's meeting is NPD," Herman Stiche said, wondering for the 23rd time why'd he'd promoted Babcock to Senior VP. "Let's move on to opportunities? Anyone?"

His gaze paused on his portrait. His avocado-green golf jacket was lost in the background of chartreuse curtains and Sherwood-green carpet. He despised golf; and his mid-swing pose was as artificial as the carved marble fireplace that belonged in the artist's imagination. Perhaps he should have gone marlin fishing as his mother had suggested. He would've looked glamorous in bleached linen and a panama hat. If he squinted, he resembled Hemingway around the eyes.

"Most people I've talked with really like our new Doggy Donuts, Mr. Stiche. I'm sure they'll be a big part of our revenue stream once we get out the bugs."

"Meat-flavored donuts for dogs are hardly an opportunity, Regina," Babcock said, muffling his grumble by reaching across the table. He dug into the donut pyramid, extracting a sugar-covered raspberry jelly donut from the fourth level without disturbing the rest. He held it up between thumb and first finger. "Now, this is an opportunity."

"Jelly Balls might be a best seller one day," Stiche ventured.

"Except they get squishy when it's humid," Leo countered, picking out a lime Jelly Ball for himself. He squeezed a green globule from the side. "There's your problem, right there."

"We're working on it, Mr. Stiche," Jeremy interjected.

He was always red in the face, as if complexion and hair color went hand in hand with tubby intransience. His chin receded, greatly increasing his likeness to a bearded Ginger Monkey. A beard could have covered his chin, even given him an arresting appearance, rather like the 19th century explorer who discovered Ginger Monkeys. However, Jeremy settled for bushy sideburns to hide his ruddy jowls; not academic sideburns, but jolly shopkeeper whiskers. Despite his whiskers, his bulging tweed jacket with suede elbow patches made him look bookish. His tie was plaid, Clan McTavish sent by mail-order from Scotland.

"The jelly mix's the problem," he continued, reveling in a subject that demanded his chemical engineering skills. "We're trying different gelatin formulations under various environmental conditions. It's just a matter of time until we get it right."

"Soggy, and it looks like bile," Leo said dryly, oozing green jelly already dripping off the napkin he held underneath.

"My kids call them slime balls. They like them though," Regina added quickly.

"Change the name and they'll be the best seller this Halloween," Pook muttered.

Dough Inc.'s major competitor, Cal Foods, launched Ghost Goo the previous year, a white-iced, fluffy-cream-filled donut that set a new record for Halloween sales. In fact, Cal Foods set the industry standard with their seasonal items, far ahead of Dough Inc.'s pink-sprinkled Easter donuts, red-and-green-jelly Christmas donuts, and nationalistic 4th-of-July donuts. Cal Foods had Mother's Day donuts, St. Patrick's Day donuts, Abraham Lincoln's Birthday donuts (with Union and Confederate flags iced on either side), and Kwanzaa donuts with gooey black cream, to name but a few.

"Let's move on to threats," Stiche interrupted, now looking queasy. "They're more important." He scrawled an abbreviated line below 'T' before he turned from the whiteboard.

"Donut, Mr. Stiche?" Ms. Wick inquired, delving into the donut platter.

She seemed to know exactly where to go to find Herman's favorite chocolate-iced cake-donuts—bottom level, right side. She took one for herself, nudged two more onto a paper plate, and passed it to him.

"I'd rather have a Puff, if you don't mind Ms. Wick."

"We're out of Puffs, Mr. Stiche. Cake has more bicarbonate, much better for indigestion."

"It's why seniors buy them," Pook peeped again. After a year with the company, Pook was still acting VP of Marketing. She sounded like a boy whose voice was starting to break. For good reason, she didn't say anything that wasn't essential to moving a conversation forward.

"Very likely, but cake always tastes stale to me. And they're chewy," Stiche grumbled.

"Donuts should melt in the mouth, tantalize the taste buds, and leave you wanting another one," Leo agreed, putting the mushy Jelly Ball aside and greedily eyeing the donut platter.

With his favorite Strawberry Puffs long gone, it was down to second choices.

"Threats, y'all?" Stiche said moodily.

"No threats that I know of," Babcock declared, folding his arms on his chest. "Interest rates are headed down, so our cost of capital will be even lower than I anticipated in next year's budget. We need to look for firms to acquire."

"That's good news, but there's at least one threat out there, Tom. Every company has threats. What about Cal Foods? What are they doing that we need to know about?"

"We ought to swallow them and be done with it," Babcock said.

He couldn't help sneering. Cal Foods was headquartered in Cleveland, not California. The name was a marketing ruse—they had aspirations for the national stage, with no money to get there. There were even unconfirmed rumors about Cal Foods outsourcing production to Mexico to save money.

"There's no point in buying them. We're outselling them two to one in every market," Leo said, looking at the two cake-donuts on Stiche's plate. "If you're not going to eat those, Mr. Stiche, I'll take one?"

"Take both," Stiche replied before he caught Ms. Wick's eye.

"They have bicarbonate," she said with a motherly head shake.

"How much bicarbonate?"

"Exactly two and a quarter cups in every hopper, Mr. Stiche, instead of yeast. Otherwise cake would be spongy," Jeremy explained, at the same time picking flecks of dried flour from the lapels of his tweed jacket.

"Our cake donuts have 0.68 percent sodium bicarbonate on average. We're right at the industry standard," Leo confirmed before starting in on the chocolate icing.

"Not many people know we're still using Marvin's original recipe," Jeremy added.

"Or that we do the chocolate icing with the same machines he bought in Germany after the war. Buying those 100 series was his best decision." Max Nussbaum searched the platter for his favorite frosting. "Anyone seen cake with vanilla sprinkles?"

"On the bottom, where they always are," Ms. Wick replied.

"I remember my father talking about them back in '48. I was eight years old when he took those babies out of the crates, set 'em out on the floor, and went straight to icing ten thousand nuts a day." Max Nussbaum pushed aside chocolate and strawberry iced donuts before he found vanilla.

"One of Marvin's wisest decisions," Stiche agreed. "Good equipment was a real advantage back then."

"We never had a single problem until we used them for honey-glazed. Big mistake! They're always breaking down; at least once a week." Max Nussbaum glared at Babcock, who'd argued against buying dedicated glazing machines.

"They wouldn't be a problem if you cleaned them more often!" Babcock said under his breath.

"We can't stop honey getting into the gears. Those new 500 series will ice just about anything."

"It's cheaper to clean what we already have, every day if you have to," Babcock snapped. "Better still, hire an outside contractor so we don't have to pay union wages."

"Try to stay on topic, y'all. Threats anyone?"

"No threats, Mr. Stiche," Babcock replied airily.

"I think we should discuss Cal Foods," Pook said, taking a very deep breath. "They have lots of new products hitting the shelves. I've heard rumors about them launching an oversized donut."

"We've been working on a new nut, just in case," Jeremy explained. He caught Stiche's eye. "A bigger Puff, actually. Nothing special."

"We need to start doing focus groups if we're going to compete effectively," Pook said, sitting up straight. She was as tall as her son, Frederick. He was 12 and gloomily dark-eyed. Everyone called him Frodo.

Babcock yawned. "With our market share, we're the best. Strategically speaking, it's more important to look at corporate restructuring."

"True and timely, Tom. We need to shake things up a bit. Put it on the agenda for the next meeting, Ms. Wick."

"Next week is about new products, Sir."

"Restructuring for the first hour, then NPD," Babcock declared.

"New products will need more than a few minutes at the end," Jeremy complained.

"I'm preparing a PowerPoint," Pook added. "I'll need at least thirty minutes."

Babcock glared at both of them. "Other priorities prevail."

Stiche cast his gaze around the table. He stopped on Pook like he usually did. Eleanor Pook was his most recent addition to the management team. She was 33, eye-catching pretty, and smart, a good hire by any standard. She was shy yet cheerful, despite being divorced for two months, and six months pregnant with her second child. She ran the Marketing Department and assisted Jeremy with new product development.

"You've been rather quiet this morning, Eleanor. Nothing wrong is there?" he inquired.

Pook shrugged—it looked like she trembled. "Nothing a few focus groups couldn't fix, Mr. Stiche."

"We sold 432 million bucks worth of donuts last year with almost no advertising budget. We're on track for half a billion this year. The only thing wrong with this company is Marketing isn't aggressive enough," Babcock said with executive exasperation.

Shell-shocked, Herman asked, "So no threats that you can see, Eleanor?"

"Other than rumors about Cal, it sounds like the only threat on the horizon is out-of-date equipment, Mr. Stiche." Pook, Wharton grad and part-time docent at the City Art Museum, took an even deeper breath. "I'm more worried about the company culture."

Babcock shook his head and sighed. "Equipment's a weakness. That's internal. So is culture, if it matters at all. Threats are external. You look at the political, economic, social, and technical environment to find threats. P E S T; or STEP if you went to Wharton."

"Thank you Harvard Business School," Leo snickered.

Nussbaum jerked up. "What about pets?"

"Any other threats? Pest, step, pets, or otherwise?" Stiche said, his stomach churning so much that he almost claimed the last of Ms. Wick's cake donuts.

"Could you use a shortened September?" Ms. Wick inquired. "S-e-p-t?"

"No threats," Babcock said, staring at Pook. "But some corporate restructuring is definitely in order."

Chapter 2.

"There are more fat babies than ever, Governor."

"Fat babies, eh?" echoed Governor Stanley B. Tubman. "Aren't babies supposed to be fat, Doc?"

'Doc' was Doctor Francine Fry of St. Vitus' Hospital for Children, professor of pediatric oncology, and self-appointed president of her eight-week-old Healthy Children Action Committee, a spinoff from her Healthy Americans for Tomorrow Action Group.

"Seven-point-five pounds used to be average at birth, Governor. I've seen babies weighing twice that."

"Thirteen pounds is humongous!"

"We're facing a crisis in the delivery room, Governor. Some babies are too big to fit on the scales."

"Crises make great opportunities, Doc, but I'm not sure I'm ready for a fat baby crisis. We just finished with the oil-spill crisis. Before that, it was school bullying."

Tubman mopped sweat from his forehead as he strode back to the golf cart for a club. He glanced at his aide, Julian Whitebread, who stood in the shade, cell phone permanently plugged into his left ear, legal-size yellow notepad at the ready.

"Darn hot for this early in March," Tubman said, stealing a glance at the curvaceous Fry.

"Global climate change is finally underway, Sir."

"It's about time."

Julian had rolled his robin-egg-blue shirt-sleeves to the elbow and pulled his fashionably powder-pink tie loose around his neck. He handed over a glass of Long Island iced tea—the Governor's special brew of equal parts vodka, gin, tequila, and rum.

Tubman burped and selected a club. "Six ought to do it."

"You might be better off with a four, Sir." Julian had read two books on golf, an online architectural treatise on the design of club houses, and subscribed to *Golf Fashion*.

Tubman sipped, surveyed the terrain, and exchanged six for four. "So what's causing all these fat babies, Doc?" he asked over his shoulder.

"Fat mothers are giving birth to overweight babies, Governor."

"Makes sense to me... only babies are supposed to be fat," Tubman added under his breath.

"You have an epidemic on your hands, Governor. Teens are 17.6 percent overweight," Fry said, her fingers checking off lecture points. "And I'm sure you know the number of fat adults and senior citizens is out of control. One in every three people over 30 needs to diet. Over 50, it's nearly 50 percent."

"It sounds like there's a pattern, Sir," Julian said, taking the Governor's glass.

"Fat from cradle to grave sounds like a job for government." Tubman turned on his heel, surveyed the terrain again, and swapped four for six. "Thoughts, Hank?"

Hank Forest was stocky, savvy, and not afraid of semantics. He wasn't born to lead, yet he made an admirable campaign manager with his ability to personalize political issues.

"Fat's a big issue with the electorate, Stan. Did I tell you about an email we received from the Block family? Their grandmother passed away last week."

"I hope you sent my condolences."

"She weighed 379 pounds."

"That's a big woman."

"Unfortunately, they dropped her getting her out of the hearse. She almost took her son-in-law with her."

"Ought to put one of those carts under the coffin and wheel her over to her last resting place."

"That's what they did. It wouldn't be an issue except the undertaker charged them an extra $800. The Blocks are understandably upset."

"Nothing I can do about it."

"I looked into it, in case the media picked up the story. You know how reporters are, Stan."

"Hand 'em a good sob story and they'll play ball every time. Make 'em search for the news, and they'll find every flaw."

Forest leaned in. "One of our donors told me two bucks a pound is the going rate for overweight funerals, plus overhead and sales tax."

"That explains the extra $800 for what's her name right there."

"Elvira Block. Even the budget funeral homes are charging a weight premium, Stan. If a reporter asks you, say it's unfair, but understandable given the need to control costs in the industry."

Again, Tubman pulled out the six, weighing it carefully. Golf wasn't his game, yet Forest insisted his job required Whispering Pines Country Club membership.

"Pay as you weigh, eh? Airlines ought to charge the same premium," he said twirling the six. "They'd be making money hand over fist in a week."

"Governor," Fry said loudly. "If you're interested, I have the latest statistics with me. They're very worrying. Your average child is 31.7 percent heavier than 30 years ago. You need to do something."

The Governor stepped farther into the shade. "Are you always doom and gloom, Doctor? What hole are we on, Julian?"

"Nine, Sir."

"I thought it was ten. Are you sure we haven't played nine already?"

"You need to take action immediately, Governor Tubman."

Tubman regarded Doctor Fry. Behind her back he might have said 'dumpy.' Her hair was pulled back to a prim bun like she'd just come from surgery. Her clothes were Florence-Nightingale austere, a grey skirt that bounced on her bony knees, a dull-ivory blouse, and a crab-inspired brooch.

"I hear you. I'm on your side, Doc. My mother's been on me about flab since she went on a diet. She tells me tubbies are running past 25 percent. One in five is a crisis in anyone's mind."

"What are you going to do about it, Governor?"

"We're on top of it. It's not ready for the media yet; we're rolling out a new initiative, Doctor." Tubman lowered his voice to state-secret level. "State-funded diets. It's Hank's idea. The Legislature's agreed to pay for porkers, to diet that is, just as soon as I figure out how to pay for it."

"My wife's been on Let Us Surf, exact same menu for seven nights a week," Hank Forest said

"That's a diet, right?" Tubman inquired.

"Lettuce and seafood, Stan. They guarantee better results than drinking sugar-free soda; however, we could've eaten at *Poulet* every night for what it cost," Forest said.

20

"See, that's the problem, right there," Tubman declared. "People can't diet when it costs more than regular food."

"My friends say Let Us Surf doesn't work like it's advertised," Julian said, sounding more haughty than normal.

"She lost five pounds."

"And it only took her a week," Tubman said brightly. "Works for me."

"Six months actually. It would've been less, but you can't eat lettuce and lobster for breakfast."

"Unfortunately, the people who most need to diet are on the bottom of the economic ladder," Doctor Fry said impatiently.

"What they need is to get off their butts and exercise. Get rid of the bulging belly with a few rounds of golf," Tubman said, swinging his six club. "Lots of fresh air and sunshine. The great outdoors. Exercise is cheaper than dieting, and you can go to the bar afterwards."

"Paying for diets wouldn't be a problem if the Legislature approved another bond issue," Forest grouched.

"Governor, diet and exercise are both important; however, I'd like to talk to you about my comprehensive program of TV ads for children. I call them Healthy Choices Commercials because they're about making healthy choices."

"It sounds expensive, Doc." Tubman's election strategy was based on budget awareness. Focus groups liked the approach, even if it meant he sometimes came across as being tight-fisted.

"Kids losing weight is a vote getter, Stan," Forest said, adopting his assertive voice. "Only last week, we got a letter from Claire Bussomfeld; she's a fifth-grader at Columbus Elementary. They set up a nutrition program, *Columbus Calorie Counters*.

They've lost five pounds, and they're learning math at the same time."

"There you go! Education's the solution! Educate. Educate. Educate. Are you sure this isn't ten, Julian? I know I used my wedge on the sand trap." Tubman waved at another group of golfers. "Have a nice day," he shouted, waving his club.

"It'll take a lot more than a few fifth graders to stop this epidemic, Governor!"

"There's no need to shout, Doc! Hank's done research that shows grass roots interventions work better than government programs."

"I agree it's an interesting anecdote, but..."

"Anecdotes win elections, Doctor!" Forest had yet to find a reporter who didn't love a good story. With enough emotional appeal, it didn't matter if the facts weren't correct.

"I'm sorry. It's very frustrating. I'm a pediatric oncologist; I spend my day looking at kids with fat butts. What's happening at Columbus Elementary is wonderful; however, it's a drop in the bucket."

"Five pounds per kid is hardly a drop in the bucket. Your average fifth grader weighs what?"

"Eighty to 90 pounds on average. The range is from fifty pounds up to one-sixty."

"One-sixty?" Julian repeated under his breath.

"So there you go, Doc. The kids are losing ten percent. Pretty darned impressive, I'd say," Tubman said with a smug smile.

"Altogether it's five pounds, Stan. They get on a set of truck scales together so no one gets embarrassed," Forest explained.

"How many kids?"

"It's not important, Stan. We'll skip over the numbers and focus on kids taking responsibility. Target the emotional component. Self-esteem building. Personal motivation. Teamwork. It's all good. This could be a win-win for us."

Stan Tubman pondered the polling potential. "The program name needs to be more striking to be a vote getter. I'm thinking *Kids Kounting Kalories*, so it sounds like something the kids came up with."

"I'm not sure that's such a good idea," Julian interrupted after he wrote it down.

Forest went on regardless. "You could visit the school next week, Stan. Hop on the truck scales with the kids, help them plan their meals. The media will suck it up, plus it fits right in with our education initiatives."

"That's a step in the right direction, right there, don't you think Doc?"

"Grass roots action is important, Governor; however, we're facing a crisis of epic proportions."

"I can't imagine a fifth grader weighing 160 pounds, can you?" Julian whispered to Forest.

"I bet you were a wimpy runt as a fifth grader," Forest whispered back.

"I can't help that I have small bones."

Doctor Fry coughed louder than she needed to get their attention. "I'm here to tell you that obesity needs a multi-pronged attack, Governor."

"I got it, Doc."

"We need a program to change people's attitudes, and whatever it takes to make companies responsible."

"That's all?"

"People won't do it on their own, Governor. I have an approach I call AIR. Action initiates. Impetus stimulates. Reaction results. Taking off those unnecessary pounds has to start with direct government action."

"It sounds good, Doc. Between you and me, though, I'm afraid it's overly complicated."

Governor Tubman defined what a good first impression should be: six foot five inches of blue-eyed, beamy-shouldered ex-College-football player who wisely chose state politics over a chance at the national leagues. Not the brightest spoon in the drawer, especially after his head injury; however, he possessed superior looks and confidence to compensate. It wasn't all roses; his 1930s-style moustache and goatee was a ploy to distract attention from his pencil-thin lips.

"Frankly, Doctor Fry, I don't fancy the chances," Tubman went on. "We're tightening the belt every day, the bad economy and all."

"This is important, Governor. The future is at stake," Fry objected.

"Even with your fat crisis, I wouldn't bet a dime on the chances. There's a state constitution blocking the highway to weight loss," Tubman said, looking for confirmation from Julian, who shrugged.

"Article Three, Governor; says you have a sovereign duty to protect the people's health, safety, and welfare. Duty covers a lot of things."

"You certainly know your constitutional law, Doctor. Better than most lawyers I know."

"How did you pass diets for the masses, Governor?" Fry demanded.

"Passing it was easy after we reimbursed the Legislature for their parking fees."

Fry thought she'd heard wrong. "You mean there were no complaints about over-reach?"

"A few busy bodies caused problems. And the tax cheats; they count every penny we spend like it's their own. We beat them in court, but it was through-the-roof expensive. We had to hire three New York law firms as consultants, didn't we Hank?"

"Twenty million in legal fees, plus another five million for Cochon and Stye; they're local attorneys. At least we got a five percent discount for paying their bill promptly," Hank said.

"My committee doesn't have that sort of money."

Tubman swung his club at thin air, again. "I hate to rush important matters; however, that important meeting I mentioned is approaching rapidly. Please make your case, Doc?"

Fry heaved a frustrated sigh. "To start with, Governor, government statistics prove that every pound overweight is a year off your life."

"So Hank's already dead?" Tubman joked, his own belly wobbling against his over-tight belt.

"Overweight people have more car accidents. Statistics also show…"

"The same statistics?"

"Different ones, Governor. There's also a strong correlation between sky-rocketing medical costs and people becoming fatter." She looked through reading glasses perched on a proboscis that was more beak than nose. "The probability of surviving major surgery decreases dramatically when a patient is overweight."

"Fat's the number one killer on the operating table, eh?"

"There are surgical complications with adipose tissue."

"You sound like my mother."

"I don't mean to. It's just that people are dying every day from eating too much."

"There you go, sounding like her again."

"Tomorrow, it could be you, Governor."

"You saying I'm fat?"

"Governor, fat people have more heart attacks, liver problems, kidney failure, acid reflux, IBS, joint problems…"

"What's IBS?"

"Irritable bowel syndrome."

"I didn't know I could die from it. How can I help?"

"There are three things you can do. First, there's my comprehensive program of TV commercials for children…"

"Healthy Choices, right? You've got my support. Excellent presentation by the way, Doctor."

"I've got a PowerPoint on my laptop to show you. It has the storyboard for one of my Healthy Choices commercials, about a little blind girl who plays the piano. She doesn't have any friends, so she eats too much and…"

"Email it to Julian. Assuming you're right about that article whatever-it-is in the Constitution, I'll have one of my staff look into finding some bucks for your commercials. This economy is a real downer. You need to know it's situation dire for those of us in government. I can't spend more than a million bucks without going to the legislature. Those legal fees sucked up my discretionary funds."

"Thank you. A million dollars is more than enough to get started. We need to do this for our children, Governor. Corporations are killing them with calories."

"You really think commercials telling kids what to eat is better than getting them to exercise?"

"Anything is better than nothing."

"Doctor, looking at me now…" Tubman struck a pose that showed his best side. "…you probably don't realize I was a chubby kid."

"He lost it when he started playing football," Hank explained. "High school and college. Two national championships. Hall of Fame."

"Goooo Sooners!" Tubman and Forest shouted together.

"Exercise and education, that's the answer!" Tubman beamed.

"There are benefits to both, Governor. Meanwhile, we're losing the battle against childhood obesity. That's why you need to take action on three different fronts. My Healthy Choices commercials are only the beginning. It's obvious most food manufacturers aren't acting responsibly. You need to bring them into line with current health thinking."

"The Governor needs examples. Can you cite a specific case, Doctor?" Forest interrupted.

"Cal Foods launched this two days ago." She opened a paper bag and pulled out an oversized donut oozing cream and custard from inside, the outside glazed and dusted with confectionary sugar.

"It's a Big Nut. It's got vanilla and chocolate crème in the center. I had one yesterday," Julian said. "Too much cream for me, but still very tasty."

27

"A Big Nut is 784 calories. That's half of your child's daily calorie intake in one donut, with zero nutritional value! It's disgusting!"

"You want us to outlaw Big Nuts, Doctor Fry?"

"Governor," she began with a sigh. She deposited the bag and donut in his outstretched hand. "You tell me after you eat it."

Tubman held up the donut and squinted underneath. "There's really chocolate crème in there?"

"A Big Nut is worth three regular-sized donuts," she went on.

"Like Strawberry Puffs?" Julian asked. He always smiled, ever since his Myers-Briggs' test confirmed that his perpetual cheerfulness was a personal strength.

"Strawberry Puffs average 410 calories. I'm talking about your regular glazed or iced donuts with jelly inside; what your average fat person consumes on the way to work every morning. A standard Boston Kreme is 250 calories. Even a plain donut is 180 calories."

"You make it sound like we need to outlaw all donuts!" Tubman blanched at the likely reaction from his staff.

"And sticky buns, and cream tarts," Forest added. He excelled at upping the ante until reasonable became ridiculous.

"Croissants are a healthy alternative," Julian suggested brightly.

"Flaky French pastry is healthy?" Forest sneered.

"Actually, a mini croissant has 114 calories; medium croissants have 230; and the big ones are over 270," Fry replied.

"You can remember all that?" Tubman said, impressed.

"What I'm hearing is Boston Kreme donuts and croissants have the same calories," Forest said testily, looking at Julian.

"Donuts are deep fried so they're full of trans fats," Fry added. "For 250 calories, you're better off with a blueberry muffin."

"What about éclairs? I've heard French food is better for you," Tubman said.

"Big Nuts wouldn't be a problem if people ate green beans and kale for dinner, like my mother serves," Julian said, momentarily diverting his gaze to a pair of squirrels scrambling through the branches overhead.

"Does she fry the kale?" Fry asked. "She needs to steam it or you might as well eat donuts."

"If frying is the problem, we should outlaw French fries," Julian suggested, inspired by Forest. His infectious enthusiasm was also a Myers-Briggs' strength, one he found difficult to keep in check.

"How about we outlaw those snotty little French restaurants you like so much? Garcon! Garcon!" Forest said, snapping his fingers for effect.

"Not on my watch," Tubman retorted. "We're not outlawing French fries, or French restaurants. It's un-American."

"Even if lives are at stake?"

"Doctor Fry, banning donuts is not going to happen. Not even Big Nuts."

"Didn't you say the state can do whatever it darned well pleases, Stan?" Forest countered.

"Entirely different! Everyone knows global warming's about the fate of the Universe."

"Governor, you don't need to ban anything right away. You begin with my Healthy Choices commercials."

"And after the commercials, then what Doc? I don't want to go off half-cocked and end up with egg on my face," Tubman said. He sat on the front of the golf cart and squeezed white and brown cream and yellow custard from the Big Nut. A glob splattered on the grass. "It does have a lot of cream, doesn't it?"

"Companies like Cal Foods need an incentive to reduce the calories in their products."

"A tax on calories, eh? Now, I like that idea," Tubman said. He licked cream from his fingers before wobbling his jaw from side to side. "You hear that cracking sound, Doctor Fry? Any idea what it could be?"

"It would be better if companies did it voluntarily, Governor. Carrots, not sticks. The private sector working for the public good," Fry said, blossoming with excitement.

"Sounds reasonable," Tubman said, turning to Forest with a smirk. "A prod from the Statehouse and leave it to the free market."

"Except market forces never work the way you want them to," Forest added. "Demand and supply screw it up."

"We all agree. What we need is a tax. That'll make them sit up and take notice." Tubman stuck out his hand. "Doctor, it's been a pleasure meeting you. We'll keep in contact. Hank will drive you back to your car." He waited until Forest and Fry left in a golf cart. "Julian, stop watching the squirrels reproduce."

Julian's head jerked back to eye-level.

"Tomorrow morning, I want you to set up a task force to look into this chubby child crisis. Bring in some university experts, community groups, and a union or two; but keep it quiet! Pick people who think like we do. No companies, unless they're non-profit. I don't want complaints about profits getting in the way."

Chapter 3

"Give me twenty!"

Rocklan Babcock promptly assumed the pushup position, prone on his belly on the living room floor. Elbows crooked out, legs aligned, his toes and hands digging into faux Persian carpet.

"One," he called as he boosted himself off the floor, keeping his body ramrod stiff

It was an almost perfect pushup, just not straight enough.

"Butt down! On your fingertips, Mister!"

"Dad, twenty's too many for fingertips."

"Thirty, and don't answer back!"

Rocklan grumbled under his breath, very quietly because his father's shiny black shoes were three feet away.

"Two." His fingers bent back as he lifted up. Down again. "Three."

"Back straight. Head up, soldier!"

He kept counting as he watched his father's shiny black shoes pace the floor, one pushup every five seconds.

"Do you want to grow into a porker like that McTavish kid?"

"No Sir," Rocklan grunted. "Twenty-one."

"This'll make a man out of you. You'll thank me one day."

"Thanks, Dad. Twenty-two."

"Physical fitness; it's what you need for success! Life's about getting on top, and staying there, son. Keep going. Being in charge starts right there on the floor."

31

"Yes, sir."

"Get fat and it's all downhill, son. You want to be the alpha dog in the kennel, don't you? That's what life's about."

"Twenty-five," Rocklan groaned. His elbows trembled; his fingers felt like they were about to snap off.

His father's cell phone chimed 'From the halls of Montezuma.'

"Babcock."

"Twenty-six..." Rocklan wheezed.

"Your butt looks like Everest. Straighten up! I don't want to see a camel hump. Make it forty!"

"It was only a donut!"

"I'm on the phone. You'll thank me one day."

"Thanks, Dad."

"You saw the article on Cal Foods? Bad PR for us, Regina. Giving their stale donuts to the homeless! Why aren't we doing that? I know what I said about selling to schools at 50 percent off. I'm talking about the really stale donuts; last week's rejects. Cal's always ahead of us. What are you going to do about it?"

"Thirty-six." Rocklan's face was beet-red, strands of sweaty blond hair stuck to his forehead.

"... I'm not interested in kids learning how to make their own donuts. You might be, Regina; I'm not! Selling product, making profit, that's Dough Inc.'s prime directive."

"Forty!" Rocklan collapsed on the floor, gasping.

"You're talking about making a teensy change, Regina. I'm talking profit maximization. Big difference! We're a universe apart! Twenty sit-ups."

"It was one lousy donut, Dad."

It was a Strawberry Puff—cream and strawberry jelly oozing out the side seduced him. Three of his friends bought them at the mall. How could he have known his father would visit the store at the same time to check up on sales? He'd gorged on it, eaten all of it in a couple of mouthfuls, including the cream, before his father saw him. Unfortunately, some of the pink icing stuck to his fingers and gave him away.

"You want to get fat? Not you, Regina. I'm talking to my son."

Rocklan rolled onto his back. Sit-ups were easier when someone held his feet. He wedged them under the bottom of the nearest Italian leather couch and stretched out, his arms crooked behind his head. With a quick breath, he started.

"One."

"Stop grunting!" His father nudged a ten-pound exercise weight across the floor with his foot. "About Cal; we're in a war with those morons, Regina. Yes, I've seen Big Nuts? You tried one? We're fighting for our very existence and you're buying the competition! The sooner you decide to play on my team, the better our chances at winning the game."

It took all Rocklan's strength to lift ten pounds with his arms all the way back. His belly muscles ached before his elbows touched his knees. Leaning back with the weight was agony, even with his feet jammed under the couch. Flopping on the floor guaranteed penalty sit-ups. After five, he thought he might die. At ten, he wished he was dead.

"Twenty," he groaned, thinking he might never talk to his father again.

His father snapped shut his cell phone. "I've got to fire that woman." He turned on his heel. "I didn't hear nineteen."

"Did it."

"Jumping jacks! Fifty!"

"Can I get my breath back first?"

"What do you think of Big Nuts?"

Rocklan tried to shrug, still sprawled on the floor. "I-I-I guess they're okay," he gasped. "M-m-most kids like them. I've n-n-never had one."

"For your ears only." Babcock lowered his voice. "They're selling like hotcakes."

"They've got a bigger market share than Puffs, huh?" There was no faster way to annoy his father.

"Not yet, but they're closing the gap every day. Old Stiche's planning a Super Puff. You ought to like that."

"More people prefer chocolate over strawberry."

Thomas Babcock, MBA, frowned at his own flesh and blood. His kid was prime fraternity material—athletic, reasonably bright, and very good-looking.

"You aren't getting pimples, are you?"

"Dad, I just turned 12. I haven't even started puberty."

"The sooner the better for football, son. Where's your sister?"

"Piano lessons."

"You mean she's wasting her time! Finish the jumping jacks and I'll take you to football practice."

"It's raining cats and dogs, Dad."

"It never rained this much when I was a kid."

"It's global climate change, Dad."

Chapter 4.

"I'll be watching from now on," Babcock said, ending his five-minute tirade on employees coming to work late.

"Who's watching you?" someone muttered.

Babcock glared around the boardroom table, stopping on Jeremy. "The next item on today's agenda is new products."

"What happened to corporate restructuring?" Leo asked.

"It's too important for a weekly meeting. We'll schedule a retreat on it. Today is new products."

"Mr. Stiche told me today's meeting was about competitive advantage," Ms. Wick pouted.

"Where is Mr. Stiche?" Jeremy asked. He'd been watching the door for five minutes.

"Competitive advantage and new products are the same thing!" Babcock declared.

"He's seeing his gastro-entomologist," Ms. Wick replied, glancing up from her notepad, already recording attendance.

"We ought to send him a get-well card," Regina suggested.

"I've got one at my desk. If everyone can stop by to sign it after the meeting…"

"There's no need, Ms. Wick," Babcock interrupted. "I'm sure Herman will be in tomorrow."

"We ought to postpone the meeting," someone said.

"No need! Competitive advantage is my bailiwick too."

"Is that with an 'i'' or a 'y', Mr. Babcock?" Ms. Wick asked, erasing with the end of her pencil.

Babcock replied with a frown. "New products," he reiterated, tapping his executive pen on his black leather executive pad. "We'll start with what've we got on the launch pad."

Everyone looked at Jeremy. He swallowed and looked hopefully at Pook. She'd said she would give a brief overview of key market segments, yet she kept her head down, clutching her coffee cup.

"Um… actually, the launch pad is empty at the moment. Everything's still in assembly."

"What's in development, McTavish?"

Jeremy took a deep breath. "The new doggy donuts are nearly ready for test marketing. We've increased the amount of meat flavoring and we seemed to have cured the flatulence problem."

"Doggy donuts," Babcock repeated, inclining his head as if he hadn't heard properly.

"They're a high priority for my department," Pook said quickly. "Our market research shows 37 percent of donut buyers have dogs," she explained, raising her voice to a squeaky whisper.

Doggy donuts were Jeremy's idea. He developed a yellow, meat-flavored donut that resembled a bone for his dog, a randy cocker spaniel named Jock. Pook was visiting for dinner when she saw Jock jump onto the kitchen table to get one. She did some research on dogs, and Jeremy added small holes in the ends of the donut, and then dipped it in dye so half was purple.

"If we make the product in two sizes, we'll get some cat owners buying them as well," she went on, even more nervous because everyone was looking at her, even Ms. Wick. "We'll have to color those blue and green, of course."

"Am I missing something?" Babcock inquired.

"Tom, cats see the world differently," Jeremy explained. "We also trying different shapes."

"Like a mouse or a bird?"

"Actually, I was thinking fish. Much easier to make."

"It's a whole new market segment," Pook added.

"More like a lot of unnecessary risk," Babcock said, looking right through her.

She continued, undaunted. "What we need is a focus group of pets and their owners."

"Even more money at risk!"

"New market segments are 20 times more likely to make profits exceeding the industry average," she muttered. According to Pook principles, facts and logic won arguments.

"Doggy Donuts have enormous potential," Jeremy added. "You ought to see my dog eat them."

He rationed Jock to five Doggy Donuts per day. Jock loved them, preferring them ten to one over mealy dog biscuits, chewy strips of dried chicken, and even pig ears.

"One dog is not a new market segment!" Babcock exclaimed, brewing distain in body language.

"I don't know, Tom. My retriever loves them," Leo interjected. "Once we refine the product, we'll take Cal to the cleaners. They put their entire R&D into Big Nuts."

"We have dog nuts and they're cleaning our clock at the high end. Puff sales are down 32 percent last week," Babcock griped. "We've got nothing that even comes close to Big Nuts." He glared at Pook, then at Jeremy.

"Anyone can stuff cream and custard into fried dough," Jeremy said, turning defensive.

"Kids love Big Nuts," Babcock fired back.

"We ought to develop a line of donuts just for kids," Pook suggested. "A focus group would…"

"What we need are donuts for seniors," Max Nussbaum said with a yawn.

He looked like a gnome, wizened with long grey hair that would've covered his ears had he not combed it back. To keep awake, he sipped syrupy black coffee from an original Stiche porcelain-china tea-cup, bearing a faded family crest and the remnants of 'Stiche Bun Company' in gold glazing.

"And exactly what makes a senior donut?" Babcock demanded, sarcasm seeking anyone over 50.

"We could make them on the 500 series…" Then, Max Nussbaum looked to Pook for help.

"A focus group would tell us," Pook tried, unable to stare down Babcock.

"Why don't you tell us instead?" Babcock said, declaring victory with a Harvard MBA smirk.

"Okay. One…" Pook raised her first finger. "We know a large part of consumers' food choices are driven by behavioral factors. Two; old people are constantly spilling their food, which might explain why they like cake donuts so much."

"Max, you don't need to raise your hand," Babcock interrupted.

"Indigestion," Max said, nodding to stay awake.

"Indigestion is part of it. Cake crumbs are easy to brush off, and there's no cream to make a mess. I can't be sure without…" Pook said, her head still down.

"… a focus group. We already have cake donuts, Pook," Babcock said. "We need new ideas!"

Everyone looked at Jeremy again.

"Um… there are anti-oxidants," Jeremy ventured. "Old people love anti-oxidants."

"We tried that last year," Babcock interrupted. "We're lucky we weren't fined by the Food and Drug Administration."

"Finding the right fruit extract, that's the problem," Jeremy said, unperturbed.

Max Nussbaum yawned before his hand arrived at his mouth. He blinked. "What's wrong with strawberry jelly? Real strawberry jelly, not flavored corn syrup."

"There are almost no anti-oxidants in real jelly, Max. Raw strawberries are chock full; cook them for three hours in sugar syrup and you have chemical slush."

"And now you're going to tell me the FDA was right about false advertising?" Babcock said abruptly.

Jeremy locked his gaze on Babcock, who'd insisted they advertise 'the only donut packed full of anti-oxidants'. "We need the right fruit extract."

"Or the right chemicals!" Chemicals were the answer when nature failed to deliver.

"I'm taking Sodium Petromyacin," Leo suggested. "Senior Society magazine said it's got anti-oxidants."

"Blueberries are better for you than petroleum by-products," Jeremy said crossly. He softened his tone. "Constipation's a problem for old people. Blueberries would help that."

"So throw in some blueberry flavoring," Babcock suggested.

"Real blueberries are…"

"Expensive!" Babcock snapped.

"You think blueberries would help gas, too, Jeremy?" Max Nussbaum asked, looking pained. At 64, gas was a growing problem.

"My third point is that old people have lots of money. We could charge more for a premium product with dietary benefits," Pook pointed out. "A focus group…"

"Waste of time! We have bigger donuts to fry," Babcock interrupted. "Ms. Wick, could we have some more tea and coffee in here?"

Ms. Wick scurried off. He waited until she closed the door.

"This Big Nut thing has Stiche in a flap. He wants a Super Puff on his desk by the close of business today."

"A Super Puff's not going to cut it against Big Nuts. They're too good," Leo said, his gaze fixed on the portraits on the opposite wall, as if five Stiche generations were watching a traitor.

"More people like chocolate more than strawberry," Babcock agreed.

"We've made Chocolate Puffs in the lab," Jeremy said cautiously. "It's basically the same technology, but we mix chocolate fudge with the same crème we use in éclairs, plus a double squirt of custard and cream. Then, we roll the donut in caramelized sugar. They're not nearly as puffy as Strawberry Puffs, but still very nice."

"Make them twice the size of a regular Puff, and you might be on the right track, McTavish," Babcock said. Everyone else called Jeremy 'Jeremy.'

"I think we should try Chocolate Puffs with a focus group," Pook suggested.

"You'll have to do better than Chocolate Puffs for a name," Babcock snapped.

"Choco Puff?" Leo suggested.

"Dull! Plus it would cannibalize Puff sales."

"It could be one word, like Chocpuff, or we could hyphenate it, I suppose," someone said.

"Choc-nut?" Leo said.

Pook sat up abruptly. "Choc-o-nut could work. It has a musical note to it. Dah, dah, dah, choc- oh – nut."

"Jeremy's talking a four-stage process with Chocolate Puffs," Max Nussbaum complained. "We'll need to add to the line, or post-process the sugar coating. Either way, it'll be expensive. Of course, if we had the 500 series machines, it wouldn't be an issue, plus we could increase production by at least 50 percent."

"Personally, I'm going for Choc Puff!" Leo exclaimed. "Two words have got punch! It gets right to the issue!"

"More tea and coffee in a minute," Ms. Wick announced. She placed another plate piled with donuts on the table and sat down, her pencil again at the ready. "What issue?"

"We'll have to buy…" Max made them wait while he yawned. "… pre-made chocolate fudge."

"Meaning they'll cost more to make," Babcock complained.

"What will cost more to make?" Ms. Wick whispered to Regina "Did I miss something?"

"Chocolate Puffs," Pook replied. "We could charge more if they were bigger…"

41

"I suppose they could be bigger, but they're very filling as they are. Lots of calories too." Jeremy might have been talking to himself.

"There goes the bottom line," Max muttered.

"Let me worry about the bottom line, Nussbum. Double the size and we can meet the Big Nut head on," Babcock concluded. "Look into it, McTavish. Those anti-oxidant donuts as well, but use Leo's sodium stuff to keep down the cost. "

Jeremy sighed, as lonely as he'd ever been since his wife ran off with an auto-electrician from New Jersey. However, Pook's encouraging smile made him glow. She kept looking at him. In fact, every time he glanced at her, she quickly turned away. He liked how the overhead halogen spotlights made her hair sparkle.

Chapter 5.

"Have you finished the fat tax proposal, Julian?"

"Yes, Sir." Julian held out a thick file.

There were damp patches under his arms—he'd hurried to the University Club after an early lunch at *Poulet*, the restaurant that everyone who aspired to leadership went to.

"It's not easy to come up with a fair system, Governor."

"Fair's not the issue. A tax creates winners and whiners depending on who wants it."

Governor Stanley B. Tubman pointed at a dowdy floral-patterned couch in front of the window. It was Palladio-inspired with giant football-scene tapestries on either side, both winning touch-downs for the home team. He picked up his red leather portfolio, the Governor's insignia and his name embossed in gold on the front, and scooted on noiseless ball-bearing wheels to sit opposite Julian.

"I see you're in white today, Julian. A very nice contrast, I must say."

His chair was stainless steel and calf skin, trimmed in ermine. It was six inches higher than the couch so he looked down on Julian. The chair was a gift from an Italian manufacturing magnate seeking incentives to locate a new factory. He kept it at the University Club to impress other donors.

"The consultant's numbers look great, Sir," Julian began, throwing caution out the Palladian-style window.

"Keep 'em busy, my boy. Cochon and Stye are big donors. Teddy Cochon played quarterback for my alma mater. Stye's son is a U-Club member, dull as a dishrag, but a great go-to guy when the campaign coffers need filling." Tubman glanced around before lowering his voice. "Always a good idea to have an insider on committees. That way we know who to blame if we need to."

"Yes, Sir."

"CYA, Julian. In public life, covering your ass is the most important thing we do. Not something they teach at college, I bet."

Julian muttered 'no sir' and opened his file. The first page was a banal executive summary, carefully phrased platitudes for public consumption. The real information was hidden five pages in.

"We have three plans, Governor. Plan A; we tax the calories directly, collected at the point of sale. Every calorie would be a tenth of a penny."

"So a Big Nut would cost what... an extra eight cents? That's not a lot."

"Nineteen cents actually, Sir."

"That would put a dent in their corporate profits."

"Actually, Sir, I might have made a miss-step. I seem to remember Doctor Fry saying Big Nuts had almost 800 calories?" Julian hurriedly scribbled on pages. "It's eighty cents, Sir."

"That's a train wreck! I suppose we could lessen the pain with a cut elsewhere," Tubman reflected.

"Plan B, we rate food products for healthiness, and tax based on the ratings. We can target unhealthy foods at higher rates, so people won't buy as much of it."

"Franny Fry would like that," Tubman agreed, looking about. "White shoes and socks too, I see."

Julian glanced down before tugging his trouser' legs over his shins. "Yes, Sir. It's the Lauren look."

"My mother says white makes me look flamboyant, so I try to avoid it. It makes you look thinner. Are you dieting too?"

"I'm on a virtual diet, Sir." Julian squared his shoulders, and rose higher.

"Making dieting a virtue! That's the kind of approach we need. It's inspirational. How many pounds have you lost?"

"On my best day; I lost eight."

"Is it easy to do? I couldn't do a diet that makes you count calories and set goals."

"Actually, you use a fat app to make yourself look fat, and then you eat and exercise virtually to lose weight. I could put it on your smartphone if you wanted, Sir?"

"It sounds too complicated," Tubman said, his attention now focused on his daily schedule.

Next, he had an appointment with community organizers, followed by a game of bridge in the member's lounge, a late lunch at *Poulet,* and the rest of the afternoon on the golf course.

"What's the Plan B bottom line for a Big Nut, Julian?"

"I'm not sure, Sir, but the price will definitely go up."

"Prices go up when we raise taxes, Julian! I want to know how much so I know what to say when people complain."

"Maybe a third higher," Julian replied, wishing he'd spent more time reviewing the plans and less time touring the Internet looking for photos of fat people and fatty foods to illustrate his report.

"That's not a lot. I'll just say we want people to stop eating things that are bad for them. That way we'll look good."

"It could be more, Sir. We need a commission to do the ratings..."

Tubman interrupted with flick of his wrist. "That'd be a good job for Fry's Healthy whatever it's called."

"Healthy Americans for Tomorrow Action Group."

"HATAG. Now, there's a lousy acronym! Sounds like an appliance manufacturer. What does she call the thingie making the kid commercials?"

"Healthy Children Action Committee."

"HCAC. That's even worse! Sounds like a cough. Why don't people think up a catchy acronym, and then work out the name?"

"I don't know, Sir. There's always Healthy Choices by itself. That's catchy!"

"We'll go with that for the overall program. The Healthy Choices Commission will be in charge, or maybe Healthy Choices Agency. Which one sounds better, Julian?"

"The last one, Sir. Agency sounds more authoritative. Good for enforcement, but there might be a conflict of interest if they also do the ratings."

"Good point. We need another name, catchy but descriptive. Like HELP, because we're trying to help; or HELF; so it sounds like health. Elves have a good reputation; what with helping Santa at the North Pole."

"HELF could stand for Health... E-something... Life... Living... Um... Foundation? How about Healthy Energetic Living Foundation, Sir?"

"Foundation is too snooty. What's Plan C?"

"It's very complicated, Sir. We assign calorie limits for different food items and tax the excess. If a company makes a product with fewer calories than the limit, it gets a calorie credit.

The companies trade excesses and credits. We facilitate the exchange in return for a surcharge."

"I like it. If it's difficult to understand, lawyers will love it; and you know what that means." Tubman rubbed his thumb and first finger together. "Plus we can justify it as penalizing bad companies and rewarding companies that make healthy snacks. What's the price of a Big Nut going to be with Plan C?"

"At a minimum four trades, it would double, Sir."

"Fry will like that! However, we'll have blow-back if companies pass the higher prices on to voters. Talk to Cochon and Stye about setting up another commission to limit price increases. Now, more importantly, what's our revenue stream look like?"

Julian exhausted relief in a rush—a Cochon and Stye accountant had highlighted those numbers in fluorescent orange. "Governor, with a ten percent surcharge, and depending on the exchange rate; we're using zero-point-six, which is very conservative."

"I hope you remembered to include fee income: testing foods, getting approvals, and certifying. It'll help fill the coffers."

"I'll check with the consultants, Sir." Julian handed over single typed page. "The bottom line over the next five years, Sir."

Tubman looked down and blinked. "You're joking?"

"No Sir. A calorie exchange is a cash cow."

"More like a friggin' herd, boy. This much money deserves a good acronym."

Chapter 6.

The McTavish kitchen was more like a cooking laboratory. Pots and pans dangled from hooks screwed into the ceiling, stacked under the cupboards, and piled on the table. On the counter was a brass beam-balance scale salvaged from the US Post Office. It measured quantities in ounces and milligrams, while old-fashioned spoons measured volume in fractions. Test-tubes competed with glass Mason jars for experiment samples, a few from yesterday, most so old they were moldy.

There wasn't much room to move around—what had once been a sunny breakfast nook overlooking the parking area of the hardware store next door was now a pantry filled with row after row of jars of cooking ingredients.

"You've got to try this, Jeff. It's not as good as a Puff, but we're nearly there," Jeremy said.

"Dad, I'm stuffed. I had one of those Big Nuts on the way home from school. They're really good."

"If you want to see 13, humor me." Jeremy sliced his latest donut creation in half.

He handed it to his son, who inspected it at arm's length. It resembled a monkey fist with knobby bulges on one side. Jeff wrinkled his nose.

"It doesn't smell that bad," Jeremy grumbled.

"It smells like..." Jeff inhaled, shook his head, and smelled again. "A barn comes to mind."

"It's better for you than a spinach soufflé. Half of your daily allowance of vitamin A, B, and C, riboflavin, and niacin.

48

High in protein. Two hundred and twenty five calories a serving. The world's first diet donut that'll fill you up for eight hours."

Jeff poked a chubby forefinger at his half. It didn't look very appetizing. In fact, he wouldn't eat it even if he was starving. It was grey and lumpy, not at all like a donut.

"What's in it?"

"Regular flour has too many carbs; it's mostly bran, plus corn flour for color, and oatmeal for texture."

"What's the goop inside?"

"Vegetable extracts and macerated tofu. It tastes better than it looks," Jeremy said as he picked up the other half.

Jeff broke off a small lump and put it in his mouth.

"What do you think?"

Jeff looked away guiltily. "It's chewy, Dad."

"I can work on the texture." Jeremy watched him chew. "Doggy Donuts taste better, right?"

Jeff hunched his shoulders. "It's dry, like a stale cake donut. Really stale. Like ancient Egypt, mummified stale." He kept chewing, pushing lumps to the side of his mouth until he had to swallow or spit them out. "It's basically boring, Dad," he concluded.

"So we add…" Jeremy prompted.

"Cream. Lots of cream."

Jeff went over to the refrigerator, a white, constantly humming relic from the days when people made ice cubes by putting trays of water in the freezer. He opened the door and stooped to look inside. He squirted a small mountain of cream-in-a-can on the plate, completely burying the remains of his half of the donut.

"I've been thinking about fillings. They've got to be tasty, but low cal and healthy at the same time," Jeremy opined, looking disgusted as his son mashed cream and donut to the consistency and color of mud.

"So use a low calorie cream," Jeff replied, spooning glutinous mush into his mouth and licking his lips at the same time.

"It makes donuts turn gooey."

"It could only get better." Jeff picked a hard lump from his mouth.

"I could brighten it up with tofu-cream," Jeremy said, his humor sagging like the waist of his pants.

"You ought to start fresh, Dad," Jeff suggested, trying to find a way to discreetly put the last piece of donut in the garbage can.

"It could use more corn flour..."

Jeff shook his head, his curly hair shockingly orange. "No one's going to eat a donut that tastes like a greasy nacho chip."

"You like corn bread."

"Get rid of the bran, Dad. It's a dead end."

"Tell that to bran muffins." After nine months of cooking, sampling, analyzing, and trying new ideas, Jeremy couldn't avoid being defensive. "Try another one. I varied the proportions."

"I don't want to spoil my dinner, Dad."

Next to the pot-filled sink, dinner's ingredients, two strips of supermarket-special, past-the-sell-by-date sirloin, were defrosting on an 'I visited Branson, Missouri' microwavable plate. On a paper towel sopping up what might have been spilled milk, but was really an infusion of baking soda and artificial sweetener, were two ears of frozen Indiana corn. Next to them was the McTavish balance-the-budget food staple, two big Idaho potatoes.

'Potatoes are great,' Jeffrey thought to himself. "Fried, boiled, or broiled, but baked is the best," he added, thinking he was still speaking to himself.

"What did you say?"

Jeff glanced up. "Potatoes, Dad."

Jeremy frowned. "What about Solanum Tuberosum?"

"Can we bake them tonight? Sour cream and chives with garlic butter would be nice."

Jeremy frowned. Then, he beamed. "You're a genius! What I need for the base is a complex carbohydrate, like potato starch."

Chapter 7.

"Good morning, y'all." Stiche counted heads all the way to the head of the Boardroom table. He dropped into his seat like a sack of sugar. "We'll kick off with Big Nuts."

"We covered some options in the last meeting, Herman," Babcock began, oozing Ivy League charm with an insincere smile.

"Cal Foods are cleaning our clock. It's time for ideas and action, not options. New and exciting, hit the donut out of the ball park ideas." Stiche swung an imaginary baseball bat. "Innovate and redefine the snack food industry. Competitive advantage, that's what this game's about."

"I've got lots of ideas, but they'll take time to implement," Babcock said boldly.

"Are we talking home run or winning the game, that's the question?"

"I'm here to win the pennant," Babcock said, looking around the table, daring disagreement.

"We're on the same page then! New ideas are important, y'all. They keep us on the cutting edge," Stiche lectured, leaning back, his immense belly and barrel chest stretching his shirt buttons to popping point. "I ought to write a book about ideas. There are good ideas and bad ideas, and ideas in the middle."

"Should I put that in the minutes, Mr. Stiche?"

"Skip the part about ideas in the middle, Ms. Wick."

"It sounds like a bestseller, Herman," Babcock agreed, on the verge of yawning.

"I'm thinking of calling it *Ideas; Top Down and Bottom Up*, or maybe *Ideas for Dough*. That'd bring in the perspective of the company, how we pioneer with every product, from inventing new creams to choosing the color of sprinkles."

"Unless you're a media star, it's risky writing a book," Leo pointed out. "I'm still trying to find a publisher for my book. *The Perfect Donut*, it's about setting quality standards in the breakfast food industry. It'll be a game changer."

"Now, there's a book I'd read," Stiche enthused.

"Risky though," Babcock agreed, deliberately yawning.

"See, right there, there's a chapter. The risk of different ideas. Dough's all about risk, y'all. Being on the cutting edge, that's how firms like ours compete," Stiche beamed. "Which brings me to Jeremy's donuts."

"Eleanor and I are rushing the release of 326, Mr. Stiche," Jeremy said.

Product 326 was dessert donuts, Jeremy's latest invention, a high-end spongy bun inspired by German pastries. They were destined for the up-scale East Coast market, Seattle, San Francisco, and the richer parts of LA. The fillings were unique, pomegranate, fig, and licorice among them.

"Good work!" Stiche exclaimed, clapping his hands loudly. "Now, all we need is a name, foreign sounding, thought provoking, unusual..."

"How about krapfen speise, Mr. Stiche?" Pook replied brightly. She'd spent hours doing research.

"Crap then what?"

Pook sank lower. "It's German for donut dessert, Mr. Stiche."

"Say it again, Pook. Roll your 'r' and put a little more nasal into it."

"Krapfen speise?"

"Much better!" Stiche beamed. "Exotic! Chic! I like it. It goes back to our Austrian roots."

"Dessert donuts are too fancy to take on Big Nuts!" Babcock scoffed.

"We ought to make mocha-iced chocolate donuts," Leo said, inspired by the caramel-iced donut he'd consumed before Stiche arrived. "With some cream inside, it would go great with coffee."

Stiche pondered. "Sounds like a doughed-up café mocha to me, Leo. Those stuck-up French pastry makers already patented it!"

"What we need is a mega-donut we can put up against Big Nuts," Babcock growled, tapping his shiny executive pen on the table and staring at Jeremy. "Before we go bankrupt."

"The wolves aren't at the door yet," Stiche said confidently. "How are Choc Puff sales going, Pook?"

Pook rallied. "We're selling thirty thousand a day in our test market, Mr. Stiche. We could do better if we had inventory, but they don't store well. A half day on the shelves and they're gooey."

"They turn to crap by lunchtime," Leo muttered.

"It's the extra size," Jeremy explained. "I think there's critical mass for a donut. Make it too big and it sucks the moisture out of the cream. We end up with dried-out cream and soggy dough. There's not much we can do to stop it."

"Cal Foods don't have the problem," Leo pointed out. "That's why people love Big Nuts."

"They have more modern equipment," Jeremy responded, pointedly looking at Max Nussbaum, who managed to sit up, his mouth gaping with a yawn appropriate to just waking up.

"Five hundreds could make bigger donuts, no problemo."

"A waste of money! If we acquire Cal, Big Nuts aren't an issue," Babcock interrupted.

"There's the Harvard solution," Regina sneered. She sat up, ramrod straight as Max Nussbaum slumped down again, nodding off with dreams of shiny new equipment.

"You've got something to offer besides snide remarks, Reggie?"

"What we have here is a marketing problem, Tommy."

"I thought everything was a community relations problem for you, Regina," Babcock said icily. "Personally, I think it's a personnel problem," he added, just loud enough that she heard.

"What would it cost to acquire Cal?" Stiche interjected, indigestion churning his mood from sour to dismal.

"Based on their sales last year, Herman, I think we could pick them up for about $400 million, plus or minus."

"We'd have size for competitive advantage," Stiche thought aloud. "It never hurts to be the big boy on the block."

"Four hundred is cheap if you consider our current capitalization rate, their asset utilization and manufacturing capacity, and our ability to make cost savings by consolidating operations." Then, Babcock sat back.

Stiche just nodded. Leo pushed his chair back from the table and folded his arms. Jeremy shook his head in disbelief.

"What did he say?" Ms. Wick whispered, stenographer's pencil poised to write.

"Nothing worth recording," Regina whispered back.

"I recommend we look into it, Herman," Babcock continued with no indication he'd overheard. "A merger would be best; that way we wouldn't have to increase our debt ceiling. If we go public and put a floor under our stock price, there wouldn't be any risk."

Babcock surveyed the room. Ms. Wick would be the first person he'd fire. Then, Regina. Then, Pook. Get rid of incompetence and rebuild the company with real MBA people.

"There's always risk," Pook said. 'Risk' sounded as if she'd squealed, 'Yyyyccchhh.'

"None worth worrying about! Six months from now Dough Inc. will be the biggest donut company in the world," Babcock said, oozing self-assurance. "Market share, buying power, price control, we'll have it all."

"If we're still in b-b-business."

Babcock just smiled. Pook was no competition at all.

"We could beat them the old-fashioned way; refit all our factories with 500 series machines, and have $383 million left over," Max Nussbaum said, waking up yet again.

"Now, there's an idea! Look into it, Maxwell," Stiche decided. He turned to Regina. "Have you heard anything more?"

Regina suddenly looked as unsure of herself as Pook did on a bad day.

"There's a rumor the Governor is setting up a commission to tax high calorie foods," Stiche explained.

"You have something to tell us, Reggie?" Babcock jeered.

"I had lunch with Julian Whitebread yesterday. He confirmed the Governor's taking on the fat epidemic."

Stiche was out of his chair and on his way to the whiteboard and the dry-erase markers.

"He ought to worry about balancing his budget."

"They're still working out the details, Mr. Stiche. All I know is it's a tax without being a tax. I really don't understand it. Something about a committee rating foods and trading calorie excesses and credits."

Stiche lumbered down the Boardroom, past the French windows.

"What I want to know is why weren't we consulted up front? I gave $2,000 to the Governor's reelection campaign for a reason. For that much we should have a seat on the committee."

Regina mumbled something about private sector companies being too self-interested to have much to offer.

"Keep on top of it!" Stiche grumbled. He picked up a washable marker. "Meanwhile, y'all, I want ideas on how to respond to this tax crap; just in case. Ms. Wick, make sure you get them down."

"I don't think I should record 'crap,' Mr. Stiche."

"Put something else then!"

"You could say 'plan', Mr. Stiche? Or 'business'? How about 'tax matter'?

"I don't think 'tax matter' conveys my real feelings, Ms. Wick. Friggin' tax debacle is more like it!"

"I definitely wouldn't put that. Is tax matter okay?" Ms. Wick said as she wrote on her pad.

"From what Whitebread said, it's already decided, Mr. Stiche. There's not much we can do," Regina muttered.

"We need solid information before we do anything," Pook muttered, looking to Jeremy for emotional support.

In the instant their eyes met, both realized it was more than a glance, 230 percent more than emotional support. Finally, Jeremy offered a weak smile and a confirming nod, and tried to think of something else besides the color of her hair. The chartreuse wall behind her brought out the red; like fire mingled with high-voltage static electricity, altogether gorgeous.

"I'll get on the phone with the Governor after we finish here," Stiche said. He wrote '1-call Gov,' in big green letters. "Ms. Wick, please make sure we always have black markers in the Boardroom."

"I have some red ones in my drawer, Mr. Stiche."

"No red! No green, not even if St Patrick's Day is tomorrow. I want black, otherwise it's like Christmas!"

"Easter's closer," Max Nussbaum mumbled, sitting up. "That'd be our seasonal donuts; blueberry for boys, strawberry pink for girls, and daffodil yellow for the in-betweens."

"Herman, I'd let the Governor know we're not happy," Babcock said, certain his mind was playing tricks on him. "Jerk the campaign contribution leash a few times and he'll sit up and beg."

"Ms. Wick, leave out the part after the leash; begging too," Stiche instructed, still unhappy with green. "Do they even make yellow markers?"

"We could use highlighters," Max suggested.

"When you call the Governor, Mr. Stiche, you should offer to help with the technical stuff. If we have some input into their output it might not be as bad as we think," Regina suggested nervously.

"Good idea. Let's assume the worse," Stiche said moodily, scrawling 'technical stuff' and 'input into output.' "Are there any more cake donuts, Ms. Wick?"

"Indigestion again, Sir?"

"I think the bicarbonate helps. Leo, did I see your hand up?"

"We could look into outsourcing to keep our costs down," Leo offered, gulping a mouthful of sugary donut. He'd eaten three donuts and was starting his fourth, a misshapen cinnamon-sugared that hadn't survived final inspection.

"We're an American company and we're staying here," Stiche said, jabbing his finger at the table.

"We could look at ways to reduce calories," Jeremy suggested.

"Diet donuts; fabulous idea! Not!" Stiche chuckled. "I'll still put it down, even though I know you're joking, Jeremy." He wrote 'diet.'

"A focus group would…"

Babcock stared Pook into silence.

"Tiny nuts."

Stiche turned back from the board. "Who said that?"

Max Nussbaum raised his hand. "It's my granddaughter's idea, Mr. Stiche. Racine thinks we should make small donuts with little holes. Since she said it, I've been thinking about market viability. If we had the 500 series machines; we could double production overnight, cut our prices by 50 percent, and sell twice as many," he said without taking a breath.

"Now that's a good idea," Stiche said, writing as fast as he could. "Ms. Wick, we need an extra whiteboard in the Boardroom."

"There's one in my lab," Leo offered. "Should I fetch it?"

"No, I'm just saying. What's next folks?"

"After Max's tiny nuts, it's difficult to come up with anything better," Babcock sneered.

"We need to work more closely with the community," Regina said. "Public opinion is important. The Governor's right; people are getting fatter…"

"Hold that thought," Stiche interrupted. "I'm nearly finished with Max. Double production overnight; the 500s are really that good?"

"The 500s could quadruple output," Max Nussbaum boasted.

"The Governor needs to understand it is not our fault if people prefer donuts to spinach," Babcock declared. "Regina has to get the message out. We aren't responsible for food choices."

"I didn't say it was our fault, Tom. We should be a good corporate citizen and help people improve their lives!"

"Baloney!" Babcock rose from his chair. "Herman, we can't roll over on this one."

"I agree. It's always best to meet challenges head on," Stiche said, looking around the room. "But Regina's also right about appearing to help until we get public opinion on our side. Advertising! That's the answer."

"Advertising?" Pook sounded even more nervous than usual.

"We'll run commercials on prime time TV," Stiche declared. "Donuts are essential to a healthy lifestyle; that's the message! Donuts at kids' sporting events, donuts while jogging, donuts rock climbing. Ms. Wick make sure you get all that down. Babcock, your kid's into sports. We can use him in some of them."

"We could have Annual Donut Awards for the fittest kids," Max Nussbaum suggested between yawns.

"Shaped like this," Stiche said, drawing a skewed square with a lopsided ellipse on the board. He added dots and scribbled 'fit not fat.' "It's supposed to be a donut with sprinkles on a plaque. Art's not my forte."

"We could hire a baseball player from the major leagues as a spokesperson. A recognized face, someone who people trust, and who doesn't do drugs; that's the key for PR."

"Good idea, Regina. You hit the ball out of the park with that one! Anyone else? Leo, I see your hand up."

"Mr. Stiche, I'm all for health, but we should be the trend setter in advertising. Cutting edge commercials grab attention; we need outrageous and thought provoking, like... um..."

"Vampires sucking jelly and cream out of donuts," someone whispered.

"Home run for Leo! Ideas, that's what business is about, y'all."

"And eliminating the competition with a buyout," Babcock added under his breath.

"We need to face this challenge as an industry, Mr. Stiche."

"Right you are, Regina. Strength in numbers. Tom, you run the meeting while I call the president of Cal Foods. Between us we'll have whatever it takes."

Chapter 8.

"They caught us with our pants down, Hank," Governor Stanley B. Tubman complained as he scanned *Poulet*'s menu and sipped Chateau Rothschild '93. "Did you see the ad on TV last night; the kids are kick-boxing and eating donuts at the same time? Now that's what I call talent"

"Obviously, we have a leak somewhere," Forest said, frowning at Julian, who conveniently turned to look for their lunch guest. "I think I'll have the Alaskan King Crab. It's on the state's nickel, right Stan?"

"Crab for me too. We'll bill it to Education. They're running a surplus after last year's tax increase. What's that new initiative?"

"Kids with Kameras, Sir"

"That's the one. Turn the little brats into reporters of social injustice. Just make sure we talk schools and technology before we finish, right Hank?" Tubman chuckled.

Julian leaped from his chair like he was stung by a Yellow Jacket. Governor Tubman started to get up too, but stopped halfway, wine glass in hand.

"I'm glad you could make lunch on short notice, Doctor Fry. Some vino? My campaign is buying. Roth '93 is as good as it gets."

Doctor Fry plopped down in the remaining seat. "I don't drink, Governor. It's bad for the liver."

"Your choice. Actually, I think the '92 Roth is better. I wanted to bring you up to date on the fat plan."

"I think it's important to be positive, Governor."

"I agree, Doc. How about program? Project?"

"It's fat that's offensive!"

"Bad day at the hospital?"

"Have you seen those donut ads on TV, Governor?" Fry demanded.

"They definitely hit the ground running, literally and figuratively. That ad with the boy skydiving and catching the donut at the last moment; that was awesome," Tubman replied, imbibing Rothschild '93 and completely oblivious to body language.

"Altogether excellent," Forest added, sampling and smacking his lips.

"It's appalling that they're allowed to show ads like that on TV, Governor, especially to kids! The message it sends is awful!"

"Now Doctor, let's not spoil a good meal with a bad mood," Tubman interrupted.

"We need to change people's behavior, Governor, not reinforce it."

"I couldn't agree more! Julian, why don't you explain the new fat tax. It'll change behavior overnight."

Fry interrupted. "I'd rather we teach people about nutrition and why they need to exercise, Governor. That'll produce long-lasting results."

Tubman barely glanced up from forcing a slab of chilled butter into a thick slice of crusty French bread. "Longer than a tax? I seriously doubt it. Taxes never go away."

"Governor, my research shows…"

"The Governor doesn't have time for a long lecture, Doctor. Maybe some bullet points that are right on target." Ready to order, Forest gestured for a waiter.

"Governor, my research shows the most effective way to change behavior is subliminal messaging on TV," Fry expounded, opening the file she'd brought with her.

"You mean like the donut commercials? They make me want to stuff myself with carbs," Forest said before he turned to the waiter. "The Governor and I will have the crab, legs not claws; they're too much work, extra sauce, and a side of pommy fritters."

"They're so blatant, they're nauseating." Doctor Fry mopped her brow, uncertain whether heat or nerves caused it. "Salad Françoise with the dressing on the side; thank you."

"Good bread, this French stuff," Tubman said, buttering another slice.

"I'll go with green, so La Françoise too. And could we have some more le pain," Julian said to the waiter before he departed.

"Governor, I called the TV stations yesterday."

"I'm glad you're taking the initiative on this, Doctor! Grass roots, you can't go wrong, right Hank?"

"The Governor's a firm believer in concerned citizens," Hank added, respectfully turning to Tubman.

"Indeed I am. My grandmother, bless her soul, always said, 'their business is my business.' She always wore green on St. Patrick's Day. There wasn't a drop of Irish blood in her. It was the same with Italy. She had a sticker on her car; 'Eat More Spaghetti.'"

Fry frowned. "I'm sure she was a wonderful person, Governor. What I learned when I called the TV stations, was there are two weeks of donut ads scheduled. A different one every night," she added, becoming impatient as Tubman buttered more bread.

"I wonder if they'll all be as funny as last night. You see that girl? Even at my best, I could never kick that high."

"They're spending a million dollars a night, Governor!" Fry protested.

"A different ad every night. Now, that's money well spent," Forest said.

"Doctor, I have to tell you the Legislature thinks your proposal's very expensive. You may have heard a rumor that the budget is over budget." Tubman leaned closer. "It's true."

"We need four or five ads so people don't get bored, that's all, Governor. Subliminal commercials can be very effective with younger audiences; only we'll have to run them for two months or more to get the message across."

"Hare and tortoise, eh? Are you wearing green, Doctor?"

"I don't think so, Governor. My plan is to use subconscious cues with pervasive social meaning."

"Too bad. I like your approach. Very invidious," Tubman said with a snicker. He fanned out the limpid green silk handkerchief in his breast pocket.

Julian leaned close to the Governor. "You meant to say insidious, Sir."

"There's a difference? Doesn't he look dashing today, Doctor Fry?"

Fry turned her gaze on the Governor's assistant, his double-breasted lime-green shiny-silk jacket and metallic-green tie more suited to a narcissistic Irish rock star than lunch at *Poulet*.

Then, the waiter arrived. "Deux Crabe Roi and et deux Salads Françoise! Bon appetite!"

"Governor, you have to do whatever it takes to convince the Legislature," Fry resumed, forking Romaine lettuce, grimacing when she discovered oily dressing underneath.

"You're preaching to the choir, Doc," Tubman said, tucking his napkin around his waist. "Money's tight right now. The Legislature doesn't mind paying for diets if I can find the bucks to pay for them; however, commercials are a different matter. Unfortunately, some people, and I'm not mentioning any names, will see them as wasteful extravagance."

"Not if we say the magic word," Forest suggested.

"That would be education," Tubman said for Fry's benefit.

Forest eyed the huge plate of steaming crab legs before him. "Butter?" he called to the departing waiter.

"It's on the way, Sir."

"It's not green is it? I don't think I could dip into green butter."

"No Sir? I'll bring some more bread. Is there anything else?"

"The bread is free, isn't it?" Forest quipped at the waiter's rear.

"I don't think so. They charge for water," Julian added.

"What about education?" Fry prompted.

"We all need it, don't we? I should add health too, just not for senior citizens," Tubman cackled. "They're bankrupting us, living forever and always wanting handouts."

Doctor Fry stiffened. "Making healthy choices is educational, Governor."

"I'm sure it is. Not that it matters." The Governor beamed across the table, crab leg in hand. "With our fat plan, the public won't be able to afford calories. Tell her, Julian."

"We're running with a combination of Plans B and C. That's a progressive tax on foods based on their calories and a rating system we still need to develop, and an exchange to buy and sell credits."

"Brilliant, don't you think Doc? It'll bankrupt companies like Cal and Dough in a year, two at the most."

"But Governor; people will lose their jobs." Doctor Fry flopped back in her chair. "If it saves a life, it's probably for the best," she muttered to herself.

"I'd like you to lead a new agency, Doctor," Tubman said, cracking crustacean leg. "Bring her up to speed on FREA while I work on this crab, Julian."

"The Food Rating and Exchange Agency. It'll be responsible for rating foods, setting calorie limits, and running the exchange. It'll be a paid position, of course." Julian stopped to fork his Françoise.

"Governor, I'm not sure this is the right approach," Fry said, wary for no reason at all.

"I think you have my salad, Doctor Fry," Julian said, reaching out.

"The Department of Health won't like it at all," Fry said with distaste.

"DOH won't mind if I use your dressing; if you're not going to use it."

"I meant they wouldn't want an outside agency doing their job," Fry said, still examining Romaine, salad dressing congealing into cheesy clumps.

"Strategically speaking, DOH will assist you," Tubman said between bites of white crab meat. "However, they're very busy doing inoculations and restaurant inspections. It's that time of the year," Tubman explained. "I know you can provide the leadership for FREA to be a success, Doctor."

"But..."

"No buts, Doc. It doesn't look good if government is always involved. Separation of powers and all that."

"A public-private partnership is more acceptable," Forest added, smacking his lips. "Good crab, this."

"Farm-raised, I expect," Julian said, forking through lettuce leaves to find olive slices.

"Are you always this crabby?" Forest sniped.

"What about my Healthy Choices commercials, Governor?" Fry asked, on the verge of giving up.

Tubman leaned across the table, chewing crab and staring at Fry's face. "You are wearing green."

Fry frowned at him and slowly shook her head.

"Yes, you are. Your earrings are emeralds."

"I hadn't noticed," she said coldly.

"Good for you! I think it's important to respect other cultures, don't you? Show the flag, I always say! What was I saying?"

"Governor, we were talking about Healthy Choices."

"Right! The doctor's memory is par excellente, isn't it Hank?"

"This crab is par excellente."

"Didn't you order just legs?" Tubman poked at a claw, shaking his head.

"Did you look at my presentation, Governor? I included outlines for the first four ads."

Julian and Forest returned blank stares. Tubman reached for the breadbasket.

"Why don't you run through the key points, Doc?"

"Certainly, Governor. The first ad has a little blind girl who plays the piano and eats too much. I was thinking of using my daughter for the part. Of course, she's not really blind, but no one will know," Fry added. "Then, there's an ad about two gay boys. Their relationship isn't working out so they substitute food."

"That's subliminal," Forest remarked.

"See, even Hank's wearing green today," Tubman said, pointing at Forest's grass-green tie with a pattern of interlocked golf balls.

"The third one's about an Asian girl whose parents are divorced, and number four is an African-American boy who can't get on the basketball team because he's Muslim. I want to reach as many audiences as possible," Fry went on.

"Subliminal and educational at the same time! I'm impressed," Tubman said.

"I realize four ads are expensive, but…"

"As director of both FREA and Healthy Choices, you'll have oodles of money," Tubman said before leaning closer, his voice barely a whisper. "My people think FREA should have a partner."

"I'm not sure I understand," Fry said after a few uncertain moments.

"It's an advisory role, so to speak. We want to have input, but it wouldn't look right if we were directly involved. Plus when it comes time to distribute funds..." Forest winked.

"I'm not sure..."

"My campaign can always use fiscal help."

"Governor, Healthy Choices is about helping kids."

"Once FREA is up and running, you can show a different commercial every night." Forest's reputation for frankness was legend. "We'd like a local company to assist you; Cochon and Stye. They'll work as consultants."

"There'll be money for professional actors, except for your little girl's spot, of course." Tubman gave a confidential nod.

"A real film crew." Forest framed a box with his hands and looked through." Lights, camera, action. Take one."

"You'll have an enormous impact on fat," Tubman added. "Everyone wins when we play by the rules."

Chapter 9.

"You'll get more exercise playing soccer than being a cheerleader, Sweetie," Regina opined.

"Mom, I hate soccer."

"Cheerleading is all about girls showing off their bodies."

"I don't want to play soccer."

"Soccer is a team sport, Honey. If people work together, everyone wins."

Regina's eleven-year-old daughter, Claire Bussomfeld—Regina kept her unmarried name—stared past her. The Columbus Elementary fifth-grade boys' football team was practicing on the adjacent field. They'd stopped for a coach's briefing. With their helmets off, only two were 'cute;' 30 percent were 'make do in a pinch'; the rest were in the 'no way I'm talking to them' category.

"Teamwork, that's what counts, Sweetie," Regina went on, kneeing down to make sure Claire's shoelaces were properly tied. She double knotted them to make certain.

"Last week, you said learning to be part of a community is what counts."

"Communities have to pull together to overcome diversity. That takes teamwork. Oops, I meant to say adversity. Mr. Stiche said the same thing in a meeting earlier this year. There's no fool like an old fool. Diversity is good so we don't want to overcome it." She looked up, taking Claire's hands in hers. "It's all about sharing our problems. Like your *Calorie Counters*."

Claire was suddenly uncomfortable in clingy soccer shorts and shirt.

"See, Sweetie, that's why *Calorie Counters* is so special. If one kid puts on a few pounds it's not the end of the world. Everyone else is trying to lose weight; so all together everyone wins. I don't mean 'wins' in a bad way, more like everyone gains. "

"I can't help it, Mom. I don't know why I'm getting fat."

"You're not getting fat! Well, you are a little bit pudgy in the thighs, but I'm sure it's hormones. Every kid thickens up before they start puberty. I know I did. What are you looking at, Honey?" Regina turned.

"He's cute, don't you think?" Claire confided, her eyes riveted on the captain of the football team.

Regina frowned. "That blond boy? He's Babcock's brat, isn't he?"

"Rocklan. Everyone calls him 'Hollywood' now he's doing the donut commercials. He's so good-looking. Don't you just love his hair?"

"He's Catholic, Sweetie."

Claire sighed dreamily. "He's going to St. Pius Middle School next year."

"Pious sounds like his father. You should always pick a boy who thinks exactly like you do, unless you want to spend the rest of your life arguing with him. Now, let's tuck that shirt in." Regina pushed a handful of red cloth under the waist of her daughter's black shorts.

"I can do it!"

"You are thickening up, aren't you?"

"I can't help it."

"Are you watching what you eat?"

"Yes!"

"How many calories did you eat yesterday?"

"I forget."

"Less than two thousand?" Regina waited. Claire nodded uncertainly. "A lot less, or a few less?"

"I don't remember."

"You're supposed to have 1400 a day, unless you play extra sports, Sweetie. Let's see, you had muesli and skim milk for breakfast, and I packed you a diet lunch. And for dinner you had vegetable lasagna, so that was 550 calories, and steamed green beans for 200, and another glass of skim milk. Do you have a calculator in your backpack? Was there anything else? Dessert maybe?"

Claire shook her head, looking guilty at the same time. "One was a sugar-free pudding. You said they don't count."

"Nothing else?"

"Um, I forget."

"Sweetie, we're a team, remember?"

"Rocklan and I had Big Nuts at the mall."

"They're good, aren't they?" Regina said, trying to be supportive.

"They're great. Much better than what Dough makes."

"Mr. Stiche wouldn't like to hear you say that, but it's true. They're very fattening, Pumpkin. Maybe you could share next time?"

Claire rolled her eyes. "Yes, mom."

"A little fat won't hurt you. It's probably hormonal, anyway. Now, you go out and kick that ball; and try to avoid Big Nuts."

"Rocklan eats them every day."

"He plays football so he runs them off. Plus he's doing commercials. He needs energy to burn."

"Why can't I do commercials too?"

"I didn't think you'd want to, Honey. I didn't say anything when Mr. Stiche asked. It's a lot of time. Days and days on the set. I wouldn't want you to give up the oboe. You wouldn't, either."

Claire stared as the football team jogged around the field, Rocklan leading, a dozen yards in front as always.

"He's so cute," she said dreamily.

"St. Pius and pimples will fix that."

"I'd like to do commercials."

"I think you'd be bored, Sweetie, sitting around for hours at a time while they get their cameras ready."

"Rocklan says acting is fun."

"Of course, he'd know. I'm sure you'd be great at it, if you wanted."

"You think I'm too fat to act, don't you?"

"Sweetie, your time is better spent playing your oboe."

"Rocklan has to go to Colorado this weekend. They're filming him eating donuts while he's rock climbing."

"How exciting is that."

"It's because his father is senior vice president, isn't it? He said his dad's going to run Dough one day."

Regina looked down her nose. "Over my dead body!"

Chapter 10.

At exactly 10:54 am of May 3rd, a day which would always be remembered in the snack food industry as CACA Day, Regina charged from her office. She spotted Herman Stiche bustling down the corridor, a voluminous white lab coat flapping behind him. She ran after him.

"Mr. Stiche! Mr. Stiche!"

"The custard machine's busted again," Stiche growled. "Why Max called me about it, I really don't know."

"I'm sure he wants to make the case for new equipment, Mr. Stiche," Regina said, catching her breath.

"All he talks about are his 500s. He ought to know all new purchases go through Babcock. That's my chain of command."

"Mr. Stiche, I've been on the phone with Whitebread, in the Governor's Office," Regina said very quietly.

She escorted Stiche back to her office and closed her door. She took a deep breath. This was her moment of glory, and she intended to relish it. Instead, she blurted, "Tubman just signed the Calorie Analysis and Control Act."

"He didn't!" Unlike his father, who folded under pressure and made himself sick with worry, Herman II always said that crisis management was his strong suit.

"He did."

"This is a disaster. Tell Babcock. No one else. I don't want people to panic."

"It's retroactive, Mr. Stiche. It took effect a month ago."

Stiche stormed out of Regina's office and rushed down the hall, shouting orders like a captain ordering 'Abandon Ship' at the height of a hurricane. "Emergency executive meeting, Ms. Wick! Ten minutes! Everyone there! Everyone!"

The executive team gathered in the Dough Inc. boardroom at precisely 11:06 am. Stiche was already engaged in heated conversation with Babcock, which quickly ended as people trooped in and took their assigned seats.

"Herman doesn't look happy," Leo whispered to Jeremy.

"He always sweats when there's bad news," Jeremy agreed, picking flecks of dried dough from his jacket lapels.

"We're missing lunch," Max Nussbaum grouched.

His mood improved dramatically when Ms. Wick carried in a platter of rejects she'd scrounged from Quality Control after morning shift ended, mostly sugared donuts and honey-glazed; the discarded Puffs already consumed by a voracious office staff.

"I saved these for you." Ms. Wick placed two plain cake donuts on Stiche's plate.

"No iced?" Stiche demanded after scanning the platter.

"Not today, Mr. Stiche. I do have your favorite English Breakfast freshly brewed."

"I'd rather have coffee," he grumbled, pushing aside the teacup.

"Tea's better for indigestion."

"Coffee!"

Ms. Wick knew better than to argue. "Yes, Mr. Stiche. Petunia's brewing a fresh pot."

Petunia was the receptionist, a beamy black lady with a Barbados accent and a voice that echoed through the corridors of Dough Inc.'s administrative suite when she answered the phone.

"The incompetent moron in the Governor's mansion just signed the fat bill. We're ruined," Stiche grumbled.

"We all feel the same, Herman," Babcock sympathized. "However, as you've always said, thinking strategically is what makes winners in difficult times."

"Absolutely right, Tom! Lead the discussion while I cool off."

With a barely concealed smirk, Babcock shoved his chair back and strode to his usual place when he gave presentations, highlighted with the French doors behind him. He straightened and squared his shoulders, sucked in his jowls, and contemplated the portraits of obesity across the room. None of them were leaders except perhaps Friedrich, a pale pastry chef from a quaint village in the Austrian Alps. He couldn't speak English, yet somehow he had managed to build a million-dollar business despite his wife's spending habits.

"I've just run the numbers. CACA nearly doubles the cost of our donuts," Babcock barked.

"It's only a ten percent tax," Regina argued.

Babcock glared down the table. Jeremy was certain he could see veins bulging in his neck.

"Ten percent's not that much," Leo interrupted. "It probably won't even affect sales."

"That's the basic tax!" Babcock interrupted.

"It doesn't sound like much, yet over the years I've learned that a penny will put a dent in your wallet," Max Nussbaum said to no one in particular.

Stiche threw up his hands. "Tell them the rest, Tom!"

Babcock waited a moment. "There's a 50 percent penalty for Category F foods; that's donuts! Then, we're allowed 100 calories per dry ounce of product. Over that, we pay for the excess. Add in the surcharge for buying calorie credits on the exchange and our prices go up by 98 percent. Plus there's a fee to get each item tested and certified."

"Thanks for figuring that out, Tom. What's the projected impact of doubling our prices on sales?"

"What sales?"

"Right! You can sit down now. Thoughts anyone?" Stiche said, looking around.

"It's outrageous." Leo plucked a donut from the pile.

"CACA's well-intentioned," Regina said, wondering if she should mention rumors about a new agency to restrict excessive price increases. "I'm sure we can work something with the Governor's office."

"Compromise is not in my dictionary!" Stiche said loudly, a few seconds from shouting.

"It's discriminatory. They're out to get us," Leo interjected.

"Marketing and PR should've spotted CACA coming," Babcock added, turning to Pook.

"Ideas!" Stiche snarled. "Not recriminations."

"Let's take advantage of a bad situation and go global," someone said, loud enough for Stiche to hear.

Blinking and shaking his head at the table, Max Nussbaum added, "Every other company is headed for the border."

"We are not relocating, not now, not ever. It's un-American!" Stiche spluttered, now red in the face.

Ms. Wick was so flustered she forgot to transcribe. Instead, she dug in her purse for aspirin, just in case.

"We need a focus group to find out if people will pay a buck-fifty for a standard iced," Pook pointed out.

"Last meeting, Max suggested making smaller donuts," Jeremy said, catching Pook's eye. She smiled faintly, which made him glow inside.

"Right! We make donuts weighing less than an ounce," Stiche said, instantly back in a good mood.

"If we had the 500 series machines, we could do it and lower our costs," Max Nussbaum said. "Who's bringing coffee?"

"Petunia, but I haven't seen her all day," Ms. Wick said.

It was widely known that Petunia divided her day among painting her fingernails, cadging donuts off the production line, and gossiping in the lunchroom. Answering the phone was a low priority; however, making coffee was even lower on her to-do list. For some reason, Stiche wouldn't fire her.

Babcock snapped. "It's prorated!"

"The coffee's prorated?" Stiche asked, frowning, now more pink than red.

"Page 258, the tax is prorated. Making smaller donuts doesn't help us."

"But if our donuts weigh less than an ounce, we should get a break, right?"

"Herman, the tax is applied using the Calorie Density Index." Babcock used the same voice when he enlightened his wife about economics. "If a donut has 40 percent more calories than a calorie-neutral food; whatever that is, it scores 140 on the CDI. They multiply the base tax by the CDI to determine the tax we pay. There's also a penalty for CDIs over 50."

"It sounds like the deck is stacked against us," Stiche complained. "Ideas anyone?"

"What if we make them fluffier?" Jeremy asked.

"There you go! Fluffier donuts. Jeremy's just full of good ideas," Stiche said, bouncing back from depression. "Look into fluffy donuts for the next meeting."

"Could someone pass the donut platter?" Leo inquired.

"We can fry the dough longer at a lower temperature," Max Nussbaum said, scratching a blotchy ear as he thrust the donut platter closer to Jeremy. "That'll fluff them up, only we'll pick up more calories."

"What about bubbling carbon dioxide through the dough before we fried them, and then zap them at high temperature. Crispy balls packed with cream, there might be a market," Jeremy suggested as he pushed the donut platter down the table.

Max Nussbaum didn't hesitate. "I'll definitely need 500 series mixers for that."

"We're already doing it with Choc Puffs," Jeremy reminded him.

Leo looked up from the donut platter. "That's why they're soggy in an hour."

"We could use carbon dioxide..." Max Nussbaum yawned.

"There's too much CO_2 in the atmosphere already," Regina responded, looking glum. "It's not right to destroy the environment just to stay profitable."

"No one's destroying the environment," Stiche said. "I like fishing and hunting the same as the next man. Other ideas?"

"On the bright side, CACA has funds for food manufacturers to convert equipment," Regina said.

"CACA?"

"The fat act, Mr. Stiche."

"Got it! How much?"

"One hundred thousand dollars."

"That's a drop of vanilla in the donut mixer."

"It's $100,000 for every item in the product line before the act passed. The items have to be different. We could get it for chocolate-iced cake donuts, and caramel-iced ones, and…"

"And vanilla-iced, and vanilla-iced with chocolate sprinkles…." Stiche stared at the portraits, rocking back and forth in his chair and nodding like a bobble-head doll. Finally, he smiled. "Max, how many different donut setups do we have, including the seasonals?"

"Three hundred and thirty two, Mr. Stiche."

"Someone look into it. Where's the coffee?"

"Should I see if I can find Petunia, Mr. Stiche?"

"Pook can go. I need you to write down our ideas, Ms. Wick."

"I think we should buy Cal Foods," Babcock said as Pook hurried out. "I've had my spies out. Everything I discovered so far is positive. They've invested all of their Big Nut profits in property, plant, and equipment."

"Why on Earth would we buy them?" Jeremy asked.

"Because now they're out of money, and with this tax crap, we'll pay a lot less."

Chapter 11.

"Dough's demanding WHAT?" Governor Stanley B. Tubman bellowed.

"They're asking for $33,200,000, Sir. It's in CACA, on page 793. Article 38, section 12, paragraph four." Julian held out the letter and took a step back as Tubman advanced, like a rhinoceros ready to charge. "The committee, it, er, it included funds for conversions, Sir."

"Conversions? Converting what?"

"There's an equipment allowance for each product. I'm sure they didn't know Dough had so many different products," Julian explained, shifting feet—his made-in-China black Boston loafers were suddenly too tight.

"Why didn't you bring it my attention? I never would've signed it."

"I didn't see it, Sir."

"You didn't read CACA?"

"I'm reading it now, Sir. I just finished page 352. It's rather slow going with 1,977 pages."

Tubman scowled, drumming his fingers on the table.

"With five lawyers on the committee it's full of legal mumbo jumbo, herewiths and therefores."

"I told you to keep it balanced. It's much better to have a teacher than a lawyer. Not as bright, and they don't make waves."

"There are two primary school teachers. One is from the school that started Kids Counting Calories."

"Excellent! We're working with the teacher who started it all!" Tubman enthused. "Getting a local folk hero is inspired!"

"She's the music teacher, Sir. She's been on sick leave since last May. The other teacher is retired, so he represents the local community as well. We also have a pregnant housewife representing the community. I thought it was very forward looking, involving future citizens."

"Even a pregnant housewife is better than a lawyer." Tubman paused, examining his assistant from head to toe. "You look good all black. Very intellectual!"

"Thank you, Sir. Actually, we had a homeless person too, only it turned out he was a lawyer disbarred for malpractice. One of the other lawyers used to be a civil rights professor before she went to work for Save Our Prairies."

"Two birds with one stone right there!"

"I'm sure the committee was thinking a spoonful of sugar would make the medicine go down, Sir. You said we should toss in a few incentives so it looks like we're helping small businesses."

"Where are we going to find the money?" Tubman said, still fuming.

"The Treasurer suggested the State Employees Retirement Funds until the taxes start rolling in."

"I thought SERFs were broke?"

"The Legislature's using them to cover the deficit," Julian replied.

"What about Investment Opportunities for Utilities? There's always a boat-load of money available for green projects. We'll borrow some of it for a year or two; say that people losing weight will be carbon-neutral."

"IOUs are what caused the deficit, Sir. The solar power stations aren't nearly as efficient as we thought they were. The payback looks like sometime next century."

"Tell the Treasurer to take it from the Education Operating Account."

"Sir, teacher's salaries are up 12 percent since last year. EOA is six weeks away from running out of money."

"Hell! The College Capital Budget, then?"

"It's over budget too, Sir," Julian crowed.

He'd warned the Governor about the College Capital Budget, even putting his fears in an official memo on Governor's Office letterhead, and signing it. His college professors told him the universities were building too many buildings, mostly stadiums and student rec centers to recruit from a shrinking pool of students who could barely afford tuition at the best of times.

"You told me CACA's a tax cow."

"It will be once it's up and running, Governor. I think we could cover it with Fiscal Stability Funds." Julian suggested.

Tubman cocked his head. "Where on Earth did you find a matching black tie and pocket handkerchief?"

"There's a shop on 12th Street that sells nothing but black clothes. Do you want the address, Sir?"

"Black doesn't suit me, not like it does you," Tubman replied. "When I was an intern in the Governor's Office, we never had problems like this. There was more money than we could spend. We gave it away to anyone who needed a handout."

"Haven't a lot of companies gone overseas since then?" Julian asked.

"Unpatriotic, that's what they are! They ought to stay here and pay their taxes. Profit hungry, Julian, that's what they are! Corporations are just conniving capitalist carnivores."

"You sound like my Political Economics professor, Sir. "

"Where does Dough Inc. get off demanding $33 million? Marx had the right idea. We ought to nationalize them. That guy in Argentina would," Tubman went on.

"I think you mean Nicaragua, Governor."

"President Noriake from wherever. The place ends in 'a,' that I do know. Unfortunately, we can't take over the company, at least not until they go bankrupt. No one has a problem if we're saving peoples' jobs."

Tubman looked past Julian. Outside, was a beautiful Spring day, crystal clear air, a cerulean blue sky, the temperature hovering in the mid-70s, too nice a day not to be outdoors.

"At the end of the day, Julian, the most important thing for a politician is to set priorities. That's what separates the corn from the husk."

"I'll remember that, Sir."

"There are times when this job wears you down, Julian. The pressure, the responsibility; I'm constantly making impossible decisions. I need to get out of the office and relax; bite the bullet and let off steam before the stress gets to me."

"Yes Sir."

"There aren't nearly enough perks in this job to make up for the headaches. Did I tell you I've been losing sleep from worrying too much?"

"I don't think so. I'm sorry, Sir."

"I know it's short notice, Julian; see if you can get me a tee-time this afternoon."

"Shall I say it's state business, Sir?"

Tubman answered with a nod. "Inform my afternoon appointments there's a change in venue. You can pick them up from the clubhouse in a golf cart. I'll need a lunch reservation too, somewhere I haven't been. And make sure they know the table's for me so I don't get billed. Now, about the Fry woman. How's her exchange coming?"

"Very slowly, I'm afraid, Sir. She's more interested in making her commercials. We may have appointed the wrong person."

"Actually, she's ideal for the job! She's concerned about other people. That's what counts, a willingness to go out of your way to help others, even if they don't want help. That's what it takes to be a good politician, commitment and the desire to stop injustice and inequality. It's all in here." Tubman thumped his chest. "The private sector is self-serving, Julian. I'm sure your professors told you that."

"Yes Sir, all the time."

"We, in the public service, sacrifice a great deal to serve the public interest. That's the difference between us and them. We live for social responsibility. They thrive by being irresponsible. Not just words, Julian, ideals with a purpose!"

"Yes Sir."

"She's pretty, once you get past her nose."

"I think Doctor Fry's married, Sir."

"Hank's been after me about image; my mother too."

Chapter 12.

"It looks like a member of the toadstool family, or something you'd find on the beach when the tide goes out." Jeff still hadn't touched it.

"It doesn't look very appetizing, does it? Maybe we can save it with pomegranate syrup," Jeremy said. He drizzled spirals of bright crimson sauce over his latest concoction, a fat fist-size ball injected with tofu-swirl-filling.

"Now, it looks like road kill," Jeff said, not even trying to hide his disgust.

"I'll look for something less gory. It's much better for you than strawberry jelly. It's full of anti-oxidants."

"Ew! It's got tumors, Dad."

"Those lumps are just dehydrated potato flakes."

"Last night's donuts weren't malignant."

"I was using powered potato starch last night. Unfortunately, it soaks up oil when it's fried. Flakes are better, but they bubble out. I'm beginning to think that potatoes are a dead end."

"It looks greasy," Jeff observed, lightly poking the donut.

Jeremy stepped back from the counter, frowning. He was a frustrated middle-aged chef with a degree in chemical engineering from a small Midwestern college better known for football and its per-capita beer consumption than academics.

"Try frying it at a different temperature, Dad."

"I've been frying since sunrise. At lower temperatures, it's fattening—two bites and you need to loosen your belt. Quick and hot is the answer, only it burns to a cinder."

"You might be able to sell them down south, Dad. Blackened donuts." Jeff ducked an imaginary blow.

Like a sculptor, Jeremy added a perfunctory squirt of cream-in-the-can to cover the singe marks before he sliced the donut in half.

"It's not half bad," Jeff decided as he bit into his half. "You can taste the potato, but not in a bad way. It's not like French fries or mashed potato."

Jeremy nodded and kept eating. It wasn't sweet enough, not by a long shot.

"Ditch the pomegranate," Jeff said with a bloodthirsty smirk, red syrup oozing from his lips.

The pomegranate syrup tasted bitter, the tofu filling was too thick, and the dried-sugar-cane-and-cranberry-juice sprinkles reminded Jeremy of Highlands' lichen, but those problems would be easy to fix once they sorted out the dough mix.

"I need to solve the burning problem," he decided aloud, masticating donut on the right side of his mouth.

"Use a pressure cooker, Dad."

"Easy for you to say," Jeremy rebuked, lifting his gaze.

The ceiling had scattered dents from his first attempt at pressure-frying a donut. With a massive boom the cooker exploded. A low-level official from the Department of Homeland Security paid a visit on the following Tuesday.

"What if you sucked out the air again?" Jeff suggested, trying to be helpful.

Vacuum frying, which Jeremy had also tried to stop his donuts from burning, accounted for the scorched wall behind the stove. That time, the cooker imploded, sucking in everything in a five-foot radius like a domestic black hole.

Jeremy twitched, the same way he did when he always had a good idea. "Nitrogen doesn't support combustion! That's the solution. I'll try it tomorrow."

"Dad, about the syrup. It's pretentious..."

"I've got something else we could try," Jeremy said, already looking for a jar, hidden among dozens on the counter. "I was playing around with Passion fruit yesterday." He scooped out a spoonful and slathered it on Jeff's finger.

Jeff licked his finger clean, and then sucked.

"It's supposed to be different," Jeremy declared.

He was proud of his latest syrup. Saucy Passion was far more flavorful than the fillings he'd invented for Dough Inc.'s dessert donuts. Passion fruit made his heart beat faster and stronger, but in a good way. It also brought out the taste of the sprinkles.

"It's good, except it's way too cerebral, Dad."

Jeff cocked his head to the side and licked his lips, already changing his mind as the words left his mouth. It made him feel... frisky.

"Late in the day it'd be perfect, just not in the morning. You need something that tastes like breakfast."

"That would be coffee? Or hot chocolate for you? Maybe I should try mocha icing?"

"Maybe." Then, Jeff shook his head. "Mocha's boring. It needs something different."

"How about caramel cream?"

Jeff just sighed. His father's caramel cream was tasty, yet dull, the sort of thing senior citizens loved.

"There's always toffee?"

"Blend them together. That'd be different, Dad."

"Like an expensive Irish liqueur. Chocolate, caramel and coffee."

"And toffee."

"Toffee with chocolate? That's a sin! We're wasting our time."

It was a father-son culinary experience, generating more dirty pots, pans, and mixing utensils than could fit in the McTavish dishwasher at one time. However, they pressed on regardless of the growing stack in the sink. They tried three types of coffee, Brazilian, Hawaiian, and Sumatran, caramel recipes from four different cookbooks, including an antiquated Mrs. Beaton that came to eBay via Australia, and a soft-toffee recipe that Jeremy's great-grandmother had used to make toffee for a toothless Queen Victoria when she visited Scotland. They blended them with unsweetened baking chocolate, a tablespoon at a time, tasting each one. Mostly, they made wry faces, the chocolate was too bitter, coffee was too strong, the caramel too creamy, the toffee too chewy. A few were close to being just right. And then...

"It's good," Jeff exclaimed. He licked the spoon clean.

"What was in it?" Jeremy demanded. He'd been writing the mixes down for four hours before he stopped and trusted his memory.

"Half-a-stick of chocolate, Sumatran coffee, Beaton number two, and three-minute toffee," Jeff said confidently. "It'd be even better if we cooked the toffee longer."

Chocolate, Sumatra coffee, Mrs. Beaton's second caramel recipe, carefully adjusted so it was still creamy but with far fewer calories, and four-minute toffee was delicious. Mixed together, and frothed with a whisk, it melted on the tongue, conquering the palate with a third of the calories of Dough Inc.'s best-selling icing. Even Jeremy agreed Saucy Passion didn't come close; however, it still wasn't right.

"It's the corn syrup," Jeremy opined. "Besides, it's poison for pudgies like me."

He headed for sugar, measuring cup at the ready. Canisters of white sugar, light brown sugar, dark brown sugar, and Jamaica Brown Crystals were on the second shelf of cupboard three. Jamaica was one step away from raw sugar, ideal for the rum-flavored filling in dessert donuts. The problem was it wasn't cheap enough for a breakfast donut. For a moment, he almost grabbed treacle.

"Honey," he muttered, diverting to cupboard four at the last moment.

Two hours hour later, after they tried making it seven different ways, they tested it again.

"This is it, Dad. It's really good. The flavors are all mixed with chocolate," Jeff said, rapidly scooping from the cup with his finger.

"Chocolate Sin will knock Big Nuts off the shelves for good," Jeremy declared, savoring the last precious teaspoon.

Chapter 13.

"How is everyone this morning?" Babcock asked before he sat down at the head of the Boardroom table.

"Where's Mr. Stiche?" Pook whispered.

"He's at the doctor's. It's his bowels again. The poor man's been sitting in pain all morning," Ms. Wick replied in her 'have a nice day' voice.

"I took Claire last week. We had a three-hour wait," Regina grumped.

"Nothing serious, I hope," Ms. Wick asked.

"Just hormones acting up. She's getting quite tubby on the hips," Regina confided. "It wouldn't be a problem if it was higher up."

"Do you mind if we start the meeting?" Babcock asked sourly, thinking his son could do a lot better than that chubby Claire Bussomfeld kid. The only good news; he wasn't gay.

"I waited four hours last Friday to see my proctologist," Max Nussbaum said loudly. "I took the brochure on the 500 series fryers with me so I'd have something to read besides family magazines."

"Actually, the average wait time is only two hours and fifteen minutes," Leo interrupted.

"Because people leave!" Regina snapped.

"We have a lot to get through this morning, and I'm sure everyone has plenty of work to do," Babcock said. He tried to smile as he looked around the room. "I think we'll start with a new product status report. McTavish, could you bring us up to date?"

Jeremy startled to consciousness. He'd had a long night. Partly accident, partly invention, but sometime around midnight he'd discovered another new icing by whipping melted caramel, tofu, and candied honey, barely able to keep his eyes open when he finished mixing the last batch. His son was sound asleep on the kitchen floor, yet he still woke him up. It wasn't perfection, though it came awfully close. Even Jeff said so; and he was next to impossible to please when it came to toppings. A tasty, low calorie topping was unheard of. Somehow, they'd done it.

"What's up with Babcock?" Regina whispered to Ms. Wick.

"Mr. Stiche had him take a Briggs and Stratton' test yesterday to see what he needed to work on to brighten his personality."

"How are the senior donuts progressing?" Babcock asked, his usual demanding tone lurking behind every word.

"We're making progress with antioxidants now we've switched to fruit extract."

Babcock scowled back at Jeremy. Stiche made the decision to switch from artificial to real after Jeremy found protein-rich açaí pulp in Brazil at $1.25 a gallon.

"We made a cake donut with almost no crumbs yesterday," Jeremy added proudly. It had been a week in the making.

Max Nussbaum glanced up from his stack of 500 series brochures. "But will it stick to my dentures, that's what I want to know?"

"Is that a common problem?" Babcock asked, glancing at Pook.

"We'd know if we had a focus group," she replied. He might as well have held out a cue card.

"You and your focus groups!" Babcock mangled a chuckle as he shuffled through a stack of monthly sales reports. "What's up with dog donuts?"

"The flavor-improved doggy donuts are selling better than we expected," Pook replied. "The average dog-owning customer buys four at time, that's if their dog is with them, otherwise it's two-point-five. We've had a few complaints about dogs being sick in the store. And one dog choked; a King Charles, I believe."

"One less rat on a string," Babcock said, trying hard to be funny.

According to an online test he'd taken, his humor quotient was statistically zero. He was making an extra effort in meetings. No one smiled, not even Jeremy, who drew the line at American Cocker—anything smaller was sub-canine, anything larger cost too much to feed, and couldn't fit behind the seats of his Triumph TR-6 sports car.

"Let's proceed to the main item on today's agenda," Babcock continued. "I've invited Julie Frick to bring us up to date on CACA. She's with Carson, Orson, and Nood. They're doing the legal work for the Cal acquisition."

"I thought Mr. Stiche said we were just looking into buying them?" Jeremy asked, not the only person at the table who was very surprised.

"This is a preliminary first step. Just due diligence in case we proceed," Babcock said, looking down his nose. "Ms. Frick, the floor is yours."

Frick was Harvard Law School in business-casual, a pin-striped knee-length skirt and a white silk top. She was hard as nails, with hair cut short like a lumberjack.

"It's pronounced Node, not Nude, Mr. Babcock. It's an Old English name, no doubt influenced by Viking raids in the 9th century," she added to justify Babcock's bewildered frown. "Over the last three weeks, I've had our research team examine CACA thoroughly. Needless to say, they've found a few loopholes, but short of moving to Canada, you have to comply," she began.

"It'd make more sense to head south," Max Nussbaum complained. "Nicer weather the closer you get to Florida." He looked around. There were a few interested faces, only one verging on enthusiasm.

"Viva Meh-i-ko!" Leo said with a grade-school Spanish accent.

"You might want to think about it. There's a lot less regulation across the border," Frick added. "No EPA to look in your sewers. No affirmative action claims. A lot of companies don't even pay taxes."

Leo nodded in agreement. "We'd pay a fortune for training, but they'll work for a handful of corn."

"Making a good donut takes more than cheap labor," Jeremy argued.

Max Nussbaum took advantage of the silence. He rose in his chair. "We'd get a big break on import duties if we purchased the 500 series and had them delivered to Mexico."

"It's not going to happen," Regina declared loudly, even though everything she'd been taught at Wharton said 'good business decision.'

"I'm sure we all know Mr. Stiche's feelings on relocating. Competitive advantage in the homeland. Dough is quintessentially American, etcetera, etcetera," Babcock said, grabbing a glimpse of Ms. Wick, who smiled appreciatively.

"We ought to go global. We'll be left behind otherwise," Max Nussbaum muttered. "Of course, if we have the 500s…"

Leo raised his hand and opened his mouth at the same time. "I ran the numbers. We could make donuts in China on our current equipment, air freight them here overnight, and cut our costs by 40 percent."

"I've done the numbers too," Max Nussbaum interjected. "We could cut our costs by 50 percent with the 500s, and increase production by 20 percent; and that's also overnight."

"Let's try to stay in our fields of expertise. As VP of Finance, I run the numbers. You inspect donuts, Leo. Max fixes equipment," Babcock said.

"I run this factory and manage five others," Max Nussbaum snorted.

"And you do such a good job too. Ms. Frick, you were about to say something important?"

"Actually, I'd finished, Mr. Babcock."

"We have to comply; that's it?"

"Unless you want to pay the fines. My recommendation is to follow the letter of the law and pass the increased cost onto your customers. That's what every other company is doing, except the ones going overseas."

"Two dollars and 13 cents for a Strawberry Puff," Pook peeped. People won't pay that much for a donut, not even a puff."

"They would for a Big Nut," someone muttered.

Babcock looked for the traitor. Dough Inc.'s biggest donut, the all-new Choc Puff, was failing miserably and everyone knew it. He'd even seen employees eating Big Nuts at break time.

"It's decided," he said flatly. "We'll make our donuts 25 percent smaller and charge 75 percent more. That ought to do it. I expect a short term drop in sales when the prices go up. A temporary glitch, but it won't be a problem."

"What if our customers don't want smaller donuts?" Pook asked.

"We'll puff them up to make up the difference. Someone was supposed to look into it after the last meeting." Babcock stared at Jeremy.

"What if it isn't a temporary glitch?" Pook persisted.

"The 500 series can do anything we want," Max Nussbaum replied, waving his brochures in the air.

"I think we should look into low calorie donuts," Jeremy suggested. "We could use more complex carbohydrates and protein-rich…"

"Don't waste your time. No one's going to buy a low calorie donut. It defeats the whole purpose," Babcock interrupted. He stared at Jeremy. "Your sole job is to stop Choc Puffs from getting stale in a day, got it? Big Nuts have knocked the wind right out of our sales. If they keep growing, they'll acquire us instead."

"Maybe we ought to spend more money on R&D and new equipment," Jeremy said, looking to Max Nussbaum for support.

The company's oldest employee suddenly snorted, twitching as he dreamed of installing 500 series machines in every one of Dough Inc.'s five factories.

"We're almost ready to test market dessert donuts, aren't we Jeremy?" Pook said, jumping in before Babcock.

Jeremy nodded uneasily. "We shouldn't give up on low-cal donuts."

"Donuts are never going to be low calorie," Babcock said, leaning forward, all but daring Jeremy to contradict him.

"There are ways of making them healthier. Different ingredients. How we cook them. I've got lots of ideas on vitamin-enhanced fillings."

"Donuts aren't health food! They aren't dessert food either, despite what you and Pook think, even with your fancy fillings. You can forget anything inside except custard and whipped cream."

"Everyone else likes the fillings," Pook said nervously.

"I don't. Donuts are dough, water, air and carbohydrates, deep fried and covered in sugar so they taste good for breakfast. Full-stop! End of discussion!"

"Donuts aren't dog food, yet doggy nuts are our third best-selling product." Jeremy could be tenacious when his ideas depended on it.

Babcock glared at him. With unruly, pumpkin-orange hair Jeremy looked perpetually unkempt, even more so when dark greasy spots covered his Clan McTavish tie. There were spots on his shirt too.

"Put everything else aside for Choc Puffs," Babcock said loudly so there was no mistaking his authority. "And no more talk about low calorie donuts. Dead-ends just confuse the issue."

"I heard the head of the CACA commission is worried about overweight kids," Regina said.

"So we'll make some tiny donuts especially for them," Babcock decided on the spot. "That'll score brownie points."

"We could make them square like that sponge guy, with yellow icing," Leo suggested.

Already on his third donut of the day, Leo examined the morning's display on the platter. It was an impossible choice, a Choc Puff fresh from the fryer, or the vanilla-iced cream-filled standard. He chose the Choc Puff despite his tight trousers.

Regina snorted. "Actually, stars would be better. Every kid is a winner. And it would make them look bigger."

"The kids?" someone asked.

"The donuts. Because of the points," she replied, holding up her fist, and then opening her hand with her fingers pointing out.

"I don't know. That sponge guy is awfully popular. It might work," Babcock agreed, repeating the hand gesture several times.

"We should be making healthy donuts," Jeremy muttered. If anyone heard, they didn't show it.

"Mr. Babcock," Pook began. "I know you don't like focus groups; however, I think we should do one to gauge the market reaction to our product ideas."

"A complete waste of money," Babcock growled, letting down his 'nice' disguise for a moment.

"At Wharton we learned that a good leader defines the problem before looking for solutions," Regina said smartly.

"A complete waste of time. If there's smoke, there's fire. Your house is going to burn down while you define the problem, Regina. My solution is grab a hose and put it out." Babcock had a conceited smile.

"Things might be bad, but they can always get worse," Jeremy muttered.

He doodled donut shapes on his notepad. Hexagons could be stamped from a dough slab with the advantage of maximum dough utilization. Stars didn't work unless they were sliced from an extrusion, and Dough Inc. only had one of those, a 200 series they'd bought to churn out heart-shaped donuts for Valentine's Day.

"A focus group might be helpful," he added after a while.

"Since when will a focus group solve a personnel problem?" Babcock snarled.

He turned so red in the face that Ms. Wick was worried he might be having a heart attack. She clutched her bottle of aspirin, wondering how one was supposed to administer the tablets in an emergency. With a glass of water? As a suppository? Push them down the person's throat with a finger?

Finally, Max Nussbaum blinked awake and coughed as he choked on a mouthful of donut. Everyone stared at him until got his breath back. He looked around the table as if he had to say something. He dropped the brochures one by one on the table.

"If we want to make fluffier donuts, the 500 series are just the thing."

"Temporary glitches or not, we still have to fix our plant and equipment problems," Regina said, meeting Babcock in a staring match.

Babcock sat back the same way that Stiche did when there was an important decision to make, rocking in his custom, carbon-fiber chair. "Tell Purchasing to get what you need. I'll clear it with Herman."

"With the 500 series, adding more air will be a breeze," Max Nussbaum said, picking up his brochures, more animated than anyone at the table could remember.

Chapter 14.

"Dr. Fry, I'm so glad you could make it," Governor Stanley B. Tubman said, getting to his feet.

She flopped into the reserved *Café Euro* booth. "I'm on break, Governor."

"Busy morning at the hospital, eh?"

"It's always busy. Constipation, diarrhea, kids with hemorrhoids; take your pick."

"You look like you could do with some perking up. Will you join me for coffee, Doctor?"

"Caffeine is bad for your heart, kidneys, and lower intestine. I only drink decaf."

"How about something to eat? These donuts look good." Tubman flipped his menu, his finger under an appetizing picture of donuts on a plate with a yellow and purple pansy on the side.

"Eight dollars for two donuts is outrageous."

"My treat, Doctor. I remember when donuts were a quarter each. That's inflation for you."

Hank Forest strolled over and took the empty seat beside Fry, occupying a foot of her personal space. She inched away, ignoring his extended hand. He smelled like he'd bathed in deodorant.

"I'm having a Big Nut," he declared after a cursory glance at the menu.

"They're fattening, and they're bad for your colon."

"Who would've guessed?" Forest grouched.

"I'm having a cinnamon-sugar," Tubman said smugly. He waved to the director of the State Employees Retirement Fund, who was headed towards the restaurant door. "I'll have the Treasurer get back to you," he called brightly. "Stupid twit lectured me on fiscal responsibility," he said under his breath.

"Your average cinnamon-sugared donut is 394 calories, Governor." Her face was pale pink like her blouse.

"How about cake donuts?" Tubman asked, scanning the menu upside-down.

"The little cake donuts are 267calories each. The big ones are over 400."

"They pack a punch in the paunch, don't they?"

"That's why they're rated 182 on the Calorie Density Index," Fry said. "You're better off with a fruit plate, though I must say that cherry pie looks very appetizing."

"We could share a Big Nut, Stan?" Forest suggested with a smirk he usually reserved for his wife.

"I'm more of a Puff person," Tubman replied. "I know you're busy, Doc, so let's get to the point. I want you to bring me up to date on your commercials."

"I was at the studio yesterday. There are three more Healthy Choices in the can, meaning they're ready to show, and another's being scripted."

"Marvelous! You know, I saw the first ad on TV last night. My heart went out to the little girl. She's your daughter, isn't she? Very pretty!"

"She's got my nose, I'm afraid."

"Wonderful acting," Tubman enthused. "Very endearing too, the way she looks into the camera and stuffs the custard cream donut in her face while she plays the piano."

Fry brightened immediately. "It's not too obvious, is it? It's targeted to girls who don't already have an eating problem. The goal is to stop them before they start overeating. The girls who already do, well we don't want to damage their self-esteem, so it has to be very subliminal."

"It worked for me," Forest agreed, visibly bored, finally making eye contact with the Governor while he stirred his coffee. He'd asked the Governor twice why he needed to be at the meeting and been told, 'I need you there.'

"The next one airs tonight," Fry went on. "The boys hold hands while they eat low-fat frozen yogurt. Gay kids are a tough nut to crack."

"I think pandering might be a problem," Forest mused.

"I think our ad will be very effective at getting the message across to minorities of all kinds."

"It sounds like you've been hard at work," Tubman said, reaching for his third sugar packet.

"So have you, Governor," Fry said with a smile, wishing she'd chosen the other side of the booth. "I enjoyed seeing you at Columbus Elementary."

"Oh that!" Tubman chuckled. "Grass roots are important to me, aren't they Hank?"

Forest nodded on cue, still wondering why Tubman had insisted he attend the meeting. With an election looming like a storm on the horizon, he had plenty to do, beginning with correcting the shortage of anecdotes about important issues.

"Helping the kids make a salad for lunch was truly inspired," Fry said.

"Just one of those spur of the moment things you come up when you work with the media as often as I do," Tubman said matter-of-factly.

Making the salad was Julian's idea. Once Forest got the story onto the newswire, it went national overnight, along with a video of the Governor cutting up lettuce and comparing low calorie French and Italian salad dressings, with 32 fifth graders looking on. There were even reports of French and Italian cable TV stations showing it late at night. The only negative was a few cooking shows sneered at his comments about the effects of creamy versus oily dressing on Boston lettuce.

"I really should have a fruit plate, but I'm a sucker for homemade cherry pie," Fry decided, finally picking up a menu.

Tubman patted his broad belly, shirt buttons pulled tight, the collar squashing his neck. "I'd go with the pie, Doc. It's got fruit. Tasty and healthy."

"What do you think of the donut commercials, Doctor?" Forest asked, leaning over to look at her menu. "The pie does look good, I must say."

"Disgraceful! 'Everything in moderation' indeed! What a terrible message to send to young people."

"The one that really disgusts me is 'you earn what you eat,' with a boy playing ice hockey and stuffing donuts down his throat afterwards," Tubman declared.

"Corporate greed at its very worst," Fry agreed. "I think I've been seduced by pie. Ice-cream or whipped, that's the question."

"I saw an ad yesterday," Tubman went on. "That same boy, only this time he was hitting tennis balls at a CACA sign. Every time he hits it, ka-ching! They're blaming the price increases on

CACA. That's flat out defiance! We set up the Excessive Prices Agency for that very reason."

"You need to get those ads off the TV immediately, Governor. Order the people in charge not to show them."

"Look into it, will you Hank?"

"I don't know what I can do," Forest replied. "Freedom of the press and all that."

"I know I can count on you. Say it's false advertising or something," Tubman said. He turned to Fry. "Can I count on you?"

"To do what?" Fry asked, suddenly suspicious.

"As you know, the Legislature just passed the Weight Assistance and Support Plan. Beginning next month, we'll pay 100 percent of an approved diet plan."

"I didn't know; however, it's a step in the right direction," Fry allowed, fanning herself with a tattered *Green Gardening* magazine. It was already fading, its vegetable dyes printed on recycled paper. "What about the fiscal crisis I keep hearing about?"

Tubman reacted immediately. "It's a gross exaggeration! We've got a shortage of money, that's true, but it's only until next year's budget."

"We're funding WASP out of SERF until the taxes start rolling in from CACA," Forest added, forgetting that he'd been sworn to secrecy.

Tubman scowled across the table and wiped his brow with his napkin. "I'm bakin' like a pig. I've a mind to tell them to turn the thermostats down."

Forest promptly beckoned to the waiter, who hurried over. "Can you turn on the air conditioning?"

"It is on, Sir. We can't go below 75. It's in the law they passed to save the environment."

"Don't you know who I am?" Tubman said, straightening his customary red 'power' tie emblazoned with the State logo.

"I'll talk to the manager." The waiter ambled off, smiling as he saw the Governor's scowl turn to daggers.

"Like I was saying, Doc, this new diet bill is going to rid us of fat once and for all. It should be a breath of fresh air on the political landscape; however, my opponents are kicking up a stink; we don't have the right; it doesn't cover healthy food, just prepackaged diet meals from a supplier that we identify, that sort of crap."

"It's for the public good! You're going to stand up for health, aren't you, Governor?"

Tubman lowered his voice. "I've got a few aces up my sleeve." He winked crudely. "By the way, I'd appreciate it if you didn't mention where the funds are coming from. Now, the reason I wanted to meet with you this morning, Doc; I'm going to apply the diet bill to school lunches. It's my wife's idea. We want schools to put kids on a diet if they're overweight."

"It's about time. A healthy diet is in the best interest of the child," Fry said, sitting forward.

"It will also excite the voters if we do it right," Tubman added, lowering his voice from 'confidential' to 'state secret.' "About how many kids are overweight, Doc?"

"The latest statistics put the number at one in five."

"We were hoping for more. Like one in three."

"It depends how you define overweight, Governor. You'll use BMI, I expect."

"BMI, that's er…"

"Body Mass Index, Governor. It's what doctors use."

"My wife tried to explain it to me," Forest interrupted. "It's too complex for the general public."

"Over 25 you're overweight, over 30, you're obese. How hard can it be?" Fry said. "If it makes you happy, use a density measure, like the Calorie Density Index."

Forest stared at her. "It works for people too?"

'It would have to be standardized for the population, with 100 representing the average healthy weight for each age-and-height group. It's unnecessarily complex, though we could compare people the same as using BMI."

Tubman scanned his meeting notes for highlighted areas. "I like the concept! Not the name, though. What if we call it 'fat density quotient'. It sounds honest. More scientific too."

"Indexes, or should I say 'indices', are so last century," Julian added brightly.

"FDQ... Actually, DQ sounds better doesn't it?" When no one replied, Tubman went on. "So, if I'm not mistaken, DQ will work like IQ." He made sure she was listening. "Once we educate the masses, everyone would know where they stand."

"You got that right, Stan," Forest broke in. "As soon as you know someone's IQ score, you know if they're Einstein or the village idiot."

Fry looked right at him. "I don't need an IQ score for that."

"You got that right!" Forest said. "I received a letter last week from a retired car mechanic. He was totally uninformed on the issues, your usual uneducated bigot. He moved here from Cincinnati, O-hi-o. He thought we were wasting taxpayer money building rest areas for migrating birds. We're talking a bonafide village idiot! Frankly, I was surprised he could write."

Unable to hide her frustration, Doctor Fry shook her head and breathed out.

"What I want to know is will FDQ identify enough fatties to make a difference, Doc?" Tubman demanded directly.

"With 100 as the average score, anything higher would technically be 'overweight,' Governor. Statistically speaking, it would be 50 percent of the population. It doesn't make any sense."

"Fifty percent! So one in two kids. I love statistics when they work in our favor," Tubman enthused.

"Only the other day, I was speaking with Susie Salmon," Forest said. "She does the stats for our education initiatives. Anyway, she was saying she could make the numbers say whatever we want by moralizing the data."

"I think you mean normalizing?" Fry interrupted.

"It'll come in handy at election time when people start talking about under-performing schools."

"I like your approach, Doctor," Tubman interrupted. "It's simple, straightforward, and scientific. No one can argue with it."

"It's not my approach. I'd much rather use BMI."

"But you won't mind if I credit you for FDQ, will you?"

"Stan, a fat density quotient still sounds too medical!" Forest said. "We've got to sell this to Jack and Jill Public. Plus it'll be expensive, all that weighing and measuring. How about a simple pinch test?" His fingers squeezed an imaginary roll near his waist.

"How about you stick with campaign management and media relations?" Fry said, clenching her fists under the table.

"Politics is what this is about, Doctor. Putting every other kid on a diet would cut the cost of the school lunch program by half, which lowers the deficit; and that means votes," Forest pointed out.

"Keep your voice down, Hank," Tubman interrupted, much louder than he should have. He looked straight at Fry. "We're just rearranging expenditures so the budget looks like it balances, that's all."

Fry nodded. "Don't forget that diet food costs quite a bit more than regular food."

"If does if it's lettuce compared to hamburgers. Cochon and Stye's accountant has assured me that standard prepackaged diet meals will end up saving us a boat-load of money," Tubman continued. "Mass production and all that."

"It's difficult enough matching the diet to the child—it's not one size fits all, Governor."

"We'll make it work. Of course, kids under 100 on your FDQ won't need to diet, so they'll pick from a range of franchise food. We'll buy that with a discount, as well."

"It's not my FDQ, Governor!"

"Free fast food is a great incentive for kids to lose weight," Forest added.

"Prepackaged foods are packed with preservatives."

"Still healthier than running cafeteria kitchens in every school in the state. We'll start closing them in the fall, perfect timing for November's election."

Fry directed her glare at the world in general, instead of Hank Forest. "It'll be next to impossible to find low-calorie, nutritional foods that children like, let alone standardize them."

"I don't know about your kids, but my kids are used to eating their meals out of a box," Forest said. "Stick a few vitamin pills in a hamburger and you have all of your basic food groups, plus kids love them."

"Media relations, Mr. Forest," Fry muttered.

"That's my point, Doc! Only yesterday, I received a letter from a single mother on the east side of town. Every meal her kids eat, it's either hamburgers or Big Nuts. What they miss from food they get in their pills."

"There's still the problem of too many calories."

"Even small hamburgers?"

"Any size hamburger."

"Hamburgers are as bad as Big Nuts, huh?" Forest muttered. "What if we low-cal fried them?"

"Governor, I need to get back to the hospital," Fry said, getting to her feet.

"Veggie-burgers?"

"If you want my advice…" She looked down her muzzle at Forest, thinking, 'fire him.' Instead, she said, "Diet school lunches are a good idea; however, you need to test your plan scientifically before you implement it."

Tubman looked up at her, wondering whether plastic surgery could undo nature's nose slip-up. "Tested how, Doc?"

"Summer vacation starts at the end of this month. There are lots of poor parents who need a place to drop off their kids."

Tubman glanced at his watch. With a golf game starting in exactly 45 minutes, he rolled his hand to hurry her on.

"My Center could run a day camp and evaluate different diet foods; however, we'll need to expedite the approval process."

"Meaning bend a few rules. Besides football, that's my forte, Doc!"

Chapter 15.

"Tofu's disgusting," Jeff said, regurgitating a mouthful of cream into the sink. He gargled twice and rinsed out his mouth.

Jeremy adjusted the flame of his chef-sized gas stove and continued whisking, sparing his offspring the lecture on tofu's potential to imitate just about anything, from the basic food groups to military-grade plastics. The trick was using flavors and thickeners and thinners to get the taste and texture just right.

However, he didn't blame Jeff for spitting out his tofu-whipped-cream. The last four batches ranged from concrete consistency to foul-smelling slush.

"It tastes okay, except it's like licking a cat," Jeff went on, making a face like a Pekingese dog.

In fact, the taste was actually quite good, almost as good as Cornish clotted cream on freshly baked scones, although the characteristic tofu-grey tint was slightly off-putting.

"One thing's certain, more vanilla can't fix it," Jeremy decided.

All good cream used vanilla extract; natural or artificial was the question. He'd tried both. Natural vanilla made his tofu cream furry. Artificial vanilla made it smell like a petrochemical by-product.

"It's the tofu, Dad," Jeff declared, his hands on hips with his nose wrinkled up. He could still taste cat fur. "Why can't we use real cream?"

"Because it's got more fat than an overfed hippo, and we're trying to make healthy donuts, Laddie," Jeremy replied with a big

Scottish grin. "What we've got here is a chemistry problem. Real cream is complex carbohydrates suspended in water and air."

"And tofu is bean turd." Jeff spat in the sink. "What's your point, Dad?"

"Bean curd is full of protein so it doesn't break up as easily. In fact, it strings on the spoon while I'm heating it, and then it clumps together when I whisk it, hence the fur texture."

"So whisk it faster, or harder, or something."

"I've already busted the blender," Jeremy admitted. He looked haggard, still in his work trousers and shirt, collar unbuttoned and his tartan tie askew. "I ought to be working on Choc Puffs instead of wasting my time with tofu-cream."

"Since when does Dough pay you to work at home?" Jeff pointed out. "Stiche ought to give you a share of the company for all your ideas."

Jeremy shrugged tiredly. "He was going to make me Senior VP before Babcock came along."

"He was also going to give you a share of the company, but Babcock stopped that too."

"I might get a few shares when we go public," Jeremy said, trying to stay cheerful.

"You never get what you deserve, Dad!"

"What it needs is faster whisking before it thickens," Jeremy muttered as he turned away. "We need something to really stir it up while it heats."

"Can't you heat it while you whisk?"

"I tried that. It made one solid lump. That's what broke the blender."

The blender still sat on the counter, its glass jug on top. It was cracked in four different spots. Inside, a football-sized ball of tofu-cream kept it from splitting apart. Jeff pressed the high-speed 'liquefy' switch. The blender screeched and belched smoke. It was the fourth blender to die in action during May, and the month wasn't over.

"Maybe you ought to buy two blenders next time?" he suggested.

"Buy it with what?" Jeremy grumped. "Listen, I've been meaning to tell you. That cooking camp you want to go to this summer…"

"Do you want me to reload the dishwasher, Dad?" Jeff asked, already opening the dishwasher door to unload clean pots and pans.

The door sagged on the right where the hinge was kaput. At least there wasn't a puddle of foamy water on the floor like there usually was

"Why do you always change the subject when I have something important to say?"

Jeff banged every pot and pan at least twice getting them out of the dishwasher.

Jeremy blinked and dabbed at his bloodshot eyes and waited until the noise ended. "Jeff, about summer camp…" he began.

"I don't want to talk about summer camp," Jeff muttered in a tone that as much as said, 'I'm really pissed off.'

He got to his knees and stuck his head into the still-warm dishwasher, reaching inside to rescue his father's favorite measuring spoon from the wastewater grill. The plastic grill was already split, thanks to a ten-inch carving knife that got out of hand.

The grill disintegrated when he tugged on the spoon. He picked up plastic splinters and handed them back to his father.

"I wonder if I can glue them together," Jeremy wondered aloud as he rearranged the grill pieces like a jigsaw.

Jeff sat back on his haunches. "We need a new dishwasher, Dad."

"I'll put it on the to-buy list, along with a blender."

"You spend all your money so you can work at home, and then you give your best ideas to Dough. You ought to get something back."

"That's not true. Mr. Stiche gave me a $500 bonus for the Puff, Son."

"It's his bestselling donut, Dad! You spend more than $500 on ingredients every month."

Jeremy had to agree; Strawberry Puffs were a year in the making, and tens of millions of dollars in Dough Inc. profits; however, he didn't say so. He stared at the dishwasher and sighed. "It's big for a blender," he muttered.

"What?"

"I could use the dishwasher to blend the tofu. It agitates and heats."

Jeff frowned at him, but Jeremy was already ripping paper towels from the rack.

Chapter 16.

"Mr. Stiche! Mr. Stiche!" Pook shouted.

She slammed down the phone, snatched a handful of papers from her desk drawer, and bolted from her office, past Petunia who was in a heated political discussion with three union organizers. She ran down the corridor as fast as she could in business high heels

She caught up to him in the lobby, a temple to Vermont marble. Grand Corinthian columns soared from a checkerboard floor of white and grey to a coffered ceiling painted with Mt. Olympus scenes: Venus and Cupid in a bizarre embrace, each with a donut in their private places, Poseidon feeding pink-iced donuts to porpoises, the entire panoply of Greek gods cavorting with donuts, some in ways that defied decency.

"Mr. Stiche," she began, searching for breath. "I'm glad you're feeling better."

"I feel like him," Herman grumped, his finger pointing up at Hercules laboring to carry a huge rack of donuts on his back. "Everyone's problems are my problems. Now it's Max! Do you know what he wants, Pook?"

"No Sir. This'll just take a minute."

She pursued him to the elevators, decorated Art Deco with brass donuts polished so brightly she could see her imperfections.

"Something about moving fryers to the fourth floor. We have raw materials on the fourth floor! You don't think he's lost his mind, do you? That'd be a pity. He's so close to retirement."

"Not at all, Mr. Stiche. Jeremy and I were talking about our new donut sizes yesterday."

"So much for Max's golden years! Our competitive advantage is out the door, Pook. Did you know sales are down another 30 percent? We're sinking faster than the Titanic," Herman complained, repetitively stabbing his finger on the elevator button.

"I know, Mr. Stiche. I gave you the sales numbers yesterday."

"Babcock said a decrease in demand is to be expected with higher prices."

"I'm afraid he's right; it's all about supply and demand, Mr. Stiche."

"Now you sound like Babcock! Maybe I should hire an economist. Have you noticed how moody Max is? I think it's his medication."

"Mr. Stiche, after my talk with Jeremy, I went to one of our Columbus stores, this morning, on the way to work."

"I do that sometimes to check up. You know what these retail people are like. They'll say anything to make a sale. Where's that elevator? I'm supposed to meet Babcock for lunch in 15 minutes. The acquisition; it's all he wants to talk about nowadays. I liked him more when we talked about football. He said he played offense as an undergrad, only I can't find him online. I don't think he was very good. He's not much of a team player."

"It was a sort of an on-the-spot focus group, Mr. Stiche. For an hour, I wrote down everyone's comments while they were at the counter." She thrust the papers at him. "It's very revealing."

Stiche scanned the first page, then the second. "They're all complaints, Pook?"

"Every last one, Mr. Stiche."

"Even the people who bought dog nuts?"

"They're angry that doggy donuts are cheaper than people donuts. The thing is, the market reaction isn't improving. It's getting worse. The more people hear complaints, the more they complain. If you look at the last page…"

Stiche flipped to the last page. "My God! Someone said that about Strawberry Puffs?"

"Those were her exact words."

"Would it even fit?"

"The next person in line went off about Choc Puffs. I had to leave. I couldn't take any more."

"You were brave to stay as long as you did, Pook. Do you think it's the same at all of our stores?"

"Actually, I'd expect it to be worse. Columbus is upper middle class. They tend to be more educated; they think for themselves; and they're polite too."

"Not from these comments."

"It gets worse, Sir. Regina told me that people are quitting in droves. Many of our best employees have left."

"Good for them. I wouldn't take insults like these either." Stiche looked through the pages. He was already late for his meeting with Babcock; however Babcock could wait. "Simply awful. We have to do something."

"I'm afraid our smaller donuts will only make it worse."

"A marketing campaign, Pook, that's what we need. Use our competitive advantage. We're on the customer's side, we're doing our best under difficult circumstances, that sort of thing."

"Babcock thinks it's just a temporary downturn," Pook said, throwing caution to the wind.

"He sees the big picture in Finance. That's what happens when you're always thinking in the future. While the rest of you are in crisis mode, he's talking acquisition and going public. Don't spread it around; yesterday we talked about opening a factory in China, not to outsource, mind you. They love fried rice so donuts will sell there. We won't make them with cream; Chinese people don't like it for some reason. You have to be aware of cultural factors when you globalize."

"We ought to do a focus group to make sure they like Dough donuts. We might need to modify our mix, as well as leave out the cream," Pook suggested.

"That's what I said. Tom assures me it's would be very expensive. He's right, of course."

"The study wouldn't have to be located in China. We track down some recent immigrants, or use college students."

"That's an excellent suggestion, Pook. It's early days yet, but I'll keep it in mind." Stiche said, knowing the motivational power of a sincere compliment.

"Mr. Stiche, I did an informal focus group on the next generation of dessert donuts last Friday. I had some friends over for dinner," Pook said cautiously.

"And?"

"The results were very reassuring, Mr. Stiche. Jeremy's Pomegranate syrup was very popular, preferred five to one over the others."

"How did Honey Splurge go?"

"It came right after Chocolate Extreme."

"I like Honey myself. Confectioner's sugar and apple crumble, ahhhh." Stiche licked his lips. "I think we're onto something with dessert donuts. Just don't tell Babcock."

"Mr. Stiche," Pook began. "With all these new products, we need to do focus groups. We're about to launch donuts for kids and no one has any idea if kids will like them."

"Every kid likes that sponge Bobby thing. My nephew watches him on TV."

"Watching cartoons and eating a donut are two different things, Mr. Stiche." Pook took a deep breath. "Mr. Babcock insisted we use lemon flavoring in the icing."

"Yellow's either lemon or banana. Pineapple has too much orange."

"Mr. Stiche, I don't know what percentage of kids like lemon icing. I'd like to find out before it's too late."

Stiche gave an executive shrug. "Kids love chocolate, but it wouldn't be right to use chocolate flavoring and yellow dye."

"I took some Lemonettes home for my kids to try," Pook said timidly.

"Lemonettes sounds like something from Motown, don't you think?"

"Frodo didn't like the icing, Mr. Stiche. Actually, he hated it. He said it was sour."

"A focus group of one isn't very helpful."

"That's why having a real focus group is so important."

"Babcock's right; they're too expensive, Pook. All those releases and medical forms for what we get back. Lawyers, state inspectors, the Health Department; it's just not worth the effort. "

"A focus group doesn't have to be expensive, Mr. Stiche. We could use Dough' kids. They're on summer vacation next week so we could easily get a dozen kids together for a day. That way we wouldn't have to involve any lawyers."

"Another excellent idea, Pook. We could do it in the Boardroom and save money. Would a day be long enough to test out all our donuts? It wouldn't look good if the kids got sick by overeating."

"A week would be better. Two weeks would be great. Then, we could fine-tune our products and test them the next day."

"And we call it an employee day care program! If it's cheap, Babcock won't care; and Regina will love it! You're full of bright ideas, just like Jeremy."

"Mr. Stiche, I think the results might be biased if the parents are nearby. We should do it elsewhere."

"Where do you have in mind?"

"We could rent an apartment and hire some college students to organize activities," Pook suggested.

"Babcock might go for that; his kid's into sports. How about your house? They could play in your backyard when they're not eating donuts."

"I might have a better solution, Mr. Stiche. I heard an advertisement on the radio while I was driving in this morning."

Stiche beamed. "We sign the kids up for shooting lessons at the gun club! That's an excellent idea."

"Different ad, Mr. Stiche. Mine was about a free summer camp starting in a week. It's to test out diet food for kids."

"Well that eliminates donuts."

"They need a control group, Mr. Stiche. If we provided the donuts…"

"I see where you're going, Pook! Another wonderful idea!"

"Statistically speaking, Mr. Stiche," Pook mumbled, even more nervous than the situation required. "We should test other brands besides our own."

"Evaluate the competition? Now, that's strategic planning! Get some insight into our competitors' competitive advantages. Steal a few ideas along the way. I would've suggested it if you hadn't."

Chapter 17.

"I'm not sure I understand why a company like Dough is interested in testing our new diet lunches?" Governor Stanley B. Tubman asked, frowning at his companions at the Governor's table in the state house cafeteria. "Do you Julian?"

Julian dropped his soup spoon with a clatter, spilling cream of broccoli on the tablecloth. "No Sir."

"Are any of their donuts low in calories, Doc? I mean are they doing this to get an inside seat at the government trough?"

Fry snorted. "The lowest are Quick Bites."

"I love Quick Bites," Julian said, dabbing broccoli florets with his napkin, mostly smearing them into the tablecloth so it looked like a patch of green algae. He covered the puddle with his napkin as if nothing had happened.

"They're good, aren't they? I could eat them ten at a time," Tubman declared. "I like your suit. Italian isn't it?"

"Yes Sir," Julian said, adjusting the cuffs of his black-and-white-striped shirt. "I think it makes me look taller, don't you?"

"More boyish, I think. I don't know why you'd want to be taller. Thicker soles on your shoes is the way to go for that." Tubman turned to Fry. "These Quick Bites are a step forward, right?

"There are 190 calories in the plain ones, 250 in sugared and honey glazed. Not what I'd call diet food, Governor!"

"So what exactly is their offer?" Tubman asked abruptly.

"They said they'll provide all the food for the camp if we use their employees' kids for the control group. I said no, of course. It's not right for kids to eat nothing but donuts for two weeks."

"Not even for a control group?"

"There's absolutely no nutritional value in donuts. Zero! None!"

"Dough's kids are not our problem, Doc. Tell them it's okay as long as they're managers' kids. If donuts are so bad for the rest of us, they ought to eat them as well." Tubman laughed till tears filled his eyes.

Fry's mouth gaped for ten seconds. "How... how...how can you say that?"

"My grandmother, bless her soul, used to say 'What's good for the goose is good for the gander.'"

"But..."

"No buts, Doc. It'd be different if the kids' parents were working class like the rest of us. Think of it as poetic justice," Tubman chuckled. "Now, how are those commercials going? I saw the one about the gay boys. It was sublime."

"Subliminal, Sir," Julian whispered in his ear.

"Oh, right! Very subliminal. The point is it was well done. It definitely conveyed the 'we're open to alternative lifestyles' message to the gay community. It makes sense now they're monogamous."

"That wasn't the point," Fry interjected.

"I'm very open-minded, Doc. Julian's getting married, did you know?"

"I didn't. Congratulations on tying the knot, Julian."

"We're eloping as soon as he graduates from high school."

"Hank's always telling me it's a good idea to build bridges with an election coming up," Tubman went on. "You can never be sure where the votes will come from, and with our fiscal problems, every vote counts."

"But Governor..." Fry interrupted.

"What did I just say about buts?

Tell me, Doctor Fry, what will the kids do at your summer camp, besides test out different diet foods?"

"The usual games and crafts."

"Just be sure the activities make for good photos when reporters are there; that's essential." Tubman directed his attention to Julian. "Ask Hank to set up a session with me and the media. I want all the networks there this time. The kids should be doing something meaningful; no face painting like last year's state fair. They made me look like a zombie."

Suddenly, Fry frowned. "You have an ulterior motive for supporting my summer camp, Governor?"

"I plead guilty, Doc. After my appearance at Columbus Elementary, my ratings went up by 12 percent. Hank thinks it's because I talked about applying math to solve everyday problems."

"Voters loved seeing the Governor teaching the kids," Julian explained.

"I could kiss babies and walk my dog for six months and not get half of that," Tubman added. "Voters are notoriously fickle, Doc, especially with the economy as bad as it is. I intend to appeal to the affected demographics."

Fry looked at him curiously.

"There will be two groups of kids at your camp, inner city kids and company kids from the suburbs, right? "

Fry nodded.

"The poor kids eat healthy food and the rich kids pig out on donuts, in the name of science, of course. We'll also have them compete at sports; just not rich-kid sports. It'll be great PR when the poor kids win!"

"A political statement's not what I had in mind, Governor."

"I thought you were interested in stopping kids from getting fat?"

"I am, but..."

"You want to send a powerful, subliminal message, don't you?"

"I do, but..."

"And you want to send a wake-up call to food companies to be responsible?"

"I'd like to, but..."

"If you're worried about taking advantage of a few rich kids, don't! Personally, I blame their money-grubbing parents. We wouldn't have this problem if it wasn't for companies like Dough."

Chapter 18.

"Dad, you're going the wrong way."

"One way streets exist so idiots don't drive into each other, Rocklan."

"But the sign?"

Babcock shook his head. "It's not like I'm driving dangerously. I can see there aren't any cars. You rather I waste a gallon of gas driving around the block?"

He turned into the parking lot across the street from St. Vitus' Hospital. It was recently repaved with fresh paint dividing up aisles and rectangles. In front of each parking space was a droopy yet colorful banner, each with a slogan from Fry's Healthy Choices campaign. With a surgeon's precision, he lined up his Lexus before 'Life is a cornucopia of decisions, make yours a healthy one.' He left the motor running, the air-conditioning running at maximum power.

"It's a weird place for a summer camp." Rocklan rotated in his seat.

There were no other cars in the parking lot. In the far corner were a dumpster and a flight of stairs that led down to a rusty steel door marked with a yellow and black 'Fallout Shelter.' Next to the parking area was a single-wide mobile home, fresh from the factory with manufacturers' stickers still on the windows. It was the Sunny Brook Farm model with a mock-gable roof, white storm shutters, a plumed cock perched on a wind arrow, and four skinny Corinthian columns in front of a narrow verandah. It didn't have the standard Sunny Brook Farm white picket fence; however, it did have rainbows painted on the sides, and a 'Healthy Choices Summer Camp' sign over the entry.

"There's nowhere to play, Dad," Rocklan complained.

An acre of paving, stunted prickly holly trees, and dry grass surrounded them. There was no shade to speak of, though the St. Vitus Emergency Center was handy for cases of heat stroke.

"Now listen, son. There's a reason why I signed you up for this camp."

"You want to bore me to death?"

"I want you to be my eyes and ears. And when they're testing our donuts, my mouth and nose too. I've got a lot riding on this week, son."

"You said I could go to dirt-bike camp because I did all those commercials."

"You will, just not for two weeks. I need to know what happens here first."

"Nothing by the look of it," Rocklan quipped before his father's stare silenced him.

"I don't trust Pook not to mess with the numbers."

"Face it Dad, you don't like Donut Girl," Rocklan snickered.

"This focus group crap is a waste of time, and that fool Stiche bought right into it. Luckily, we can take advantage. All the Dough executives are sending their kids. I want you to hang out with them," Babcock ordered.

"You want me to tell you what they say about you?" Rocklan asked pointedly.

"About me, about the company, about Stiche; whatever kids talk about. Mostly, I'm interested in McTavish and Pook. They've both got boys about your age. And Regina's kid too, whatever her name is."

"Claire Bussomfeld. I'm not spying on her, Dad."

"You will if you want to go to dirt-bike camp," Babcock said.

He looked Rocklan in the eye, who promptly turned away, more interested in reading the banners in the parking lot. Left to right, the next one was 'Eat right, tummy tight.' After that came, 'Today's jelly roll is tomorrow's fat roll,' 'Think before you eat meat,' 'Stay trim, look slim,' and 'There are no fat rabbits so eat carrots.'

"I'm taking over the leadership before the end of the year. The more dirt I have on the opposition, the easier it's going to be."

"You want dirt, and I want a dirt-bike." Rocklan examined his chewed fingernails. "Yamaha 125. That'll be fire-engine-red, by the way."

"It's yours if you get me what I need. However, it's got to be good dirt, not your garden-variety dirt, a lot worse than pinching pens from stationary supplies cupboard."

"Dirty dirt, huh?"

An elderly, green, British sports car rattled up next to the Lexus, spluttered, and stopped. Jeremy McTavish and his son were like pink-faced marshmallows squashed into the little cockpit. They wore the same tartan shirt, the same slouchy English cap, listening to music that belonged in a 1960s Liverpool pub.

"Conceited clown," Babcock muttered. "Always blowing his own horn."

On cue, McTavish tooted the Triumph's horn and waved good-naturedly. "It seems like we're the first ones here, Tom."

Babcock nodded grimly and studied his watch rather than speak to Stiche's favorite. It was one of those watches that pilots wore—three different time zone dials, a compass, and an altimeter, and it was waterproof to 500 meters below sea level, in case the plane crashed.

"I want lots of dirt on him for a Yamaha 125," he whispered.

Rocklan nodded obediently. He'd make it up if he had to.

Then, the next car arrived, a 1993 black Cadillac with scrapes on the side and wheels that looked like they were still turning even after the car stopped. It disgorged four noisy black kids, and left with a squeal.

Doctor Fry and three med-student-assistants departed St. Vitus. The assistants were dressed in surgical green with clipboards under their arms, each with a sign, 'Team Protein A-K', Team Vitamin L-Z', and 'Team Carbohydrate' with 'Dough Inc.' in brackets beneath. Doctor Fry wore a professional pants suit, creamy linen for summer.

The next car was Regina Kings' two-door Beemer, with a very-pregnant Pook in the passenger seat; and Claire and Pook's son, Frodo, like an elf in the rear. After that, came a steady stream of cars, pickups, sedans, and a Harley motorcycle painted marshmallow pink.

"This'll be a good experience for you to see how the other half lives, Honey," Regina said, wiping sweat from her brow prior to a casual, yet meaningful wave at the motorcycle.

She guided her daughter to the front of a queue of parents and 60 milling preteens before she spotted Babcock in heated discussion with a med-student-assistant, something about signing a legal liability waiver. Babcock's son was picking through a pile of green T-shirts.

"I'd stay with you, Sweetie, only I have to get back to the office," Regina said suddenly.

Claire stared at Rocklan in red-satin soccer shorts, a virginal-white sleeveless T-shirt, and metallic bronze sunglasses, and upped his cuteness score to eleven.

"You're in the Dough group. With all those donuts, you'll be tempted to eat too much. You'll have to keep telling yourself you're on a diet," Regina babbled, trying to eavesdrop on Pook and McTavish at the same time; however, they were too far away.

"I told the staff to break Dough's team into two groups," Pook explained quietly. "I made sure our kids will be together."

"Do they know the plan?" Jeremy asked.

"No one knows but the two of us," Pook replied. "You did a great job. I can't tell the difference, at least not by looking at them."

"I took two weeks of vacation so I can make refinements," Jeremy said, yawning. "Jeffrey ate a 236 in the car. He thinks the cream needs to be smoother."

A '236' was his notation. 'Two' for a donut mix of tofu, bran, potato-flour, and barley-whet, 'three' for a natural caramel and honey infusion that formed tasty veins through the dough, and 'six' for cinnamon-tofu-cream, which filled the center. He'd worked all night to make two dozen of them, the last one just before dawn.

"I want to be in the same group as Rocklan," Claire demanded, when the med-student-assistant gave her an extra-large purple-grape 'I make Healthy Choices' T-shirt.

Rocklan now wore an iridescent-green T-shirt. It was so tight he looked like a high-octane superhero, visibly bored as his father gave last minute instructions.

The med-student-assistant scanned his schedule of names and shrugged. No one told him why there were two groups in the Dough Inc. team. The other teams didn't have sub-groups. The

'Protein' kids all wore 'apple-red' T-shirts and the 'Vitamin' kids looked like bananas.

However, he'd been trained in conflict management, part of Respectful Relationships, a mandatory class at the university. He found an extra-large iridescent-green shirt and handed it over. "Have a good day. Remember to make healthy choices."

Chapter 19.

"I know it's only been two days, but how's the summer camp going?" Stiche asked when all of the executive committee had taken their seats.

"Swimmingly, Sir," Pook replied, not adding that there'd been a near emergency when one of the 'Protein' boys was involuntarily submerged at the local Y pool, taking his next breath a minute after the lifeguard arrived.

"Anything to report on our new donuts?"

"The kids seem to like them, Sir," Pook said, exercising her usual caution as Babcock leaned closer.

"Rocklan loves our kid donuts," Babcock added.

"Claire thinks the icing is bitter," Regina said tartly.

"I rather like Lemonettes myself," Stiche interjected. "I hate the name though. It sounds like Motown in the 60s."

Leo licked pink icing from his fingers. He was in the mood for another Strawberry Puff, yet the top one on the platter looked like it had fallen on the floor.

"My daughter, Olivia, said the icing is like sweet and sour Chinese food. You're never sure which one it is."

Babcock shot Pook a 'sore loser' look. "We probably should get started, Herman. There's a lot to cover today."

Stiche gave a cursory wave. "Ms. Wick, could you dig me out a couple of dessert donuts, please?"

"Cake donuts would be better for your indigestion, Sir."

"I just love Jeremy's pomegranate syrup." He smacked his lips in anticipation. "Delicious! The fig jam isn't nearly as good."

"The licorice isn't bad either," Leo added, still peering at the donut tray. He couldn't see any of the characteristic black filling.

"Licorice sticks in my dentures," Max Nussbaum complained. "It's bad for the machinery too. It gunks up the 500s' injectors. I've got a call in to the manufacturer."

"The first item on today's agenda is the Cal Foods acquisition," Babcock interrupted. "It's progressing nicely. They have bigger problems than we do with the fat tax, which mean they're open for bids. Their Big Nuts are still selling okay; however, the rest of their sales are down by 40 percent. I've adjusted our offer accordingly."

"What are we offering?" Regina demanded.

"I'm not at liberty to say at this time."

"It's all very hush-hush," Stiche added. He folded his hands and contemplated the table before he looked up. "I think it's time we told them the plan, Tom. However, I need everyone to promise that it won't leave this room."

"What about Jeremy?" Pook asked before she nodded.

"I'll tell him when he gets back from vacation," Stiche replied. He nodded to Babcock.

"We're going public at the end of the month," Babcock said, expecting surprise because the end of the month was less than two weeks away.

No one spoke. Regina and Pook exchanged glum glances, both thinking how unfortunate it was that Jeremy wasn't there.

"Timing is everything," Babcock went on. "Right now, the price of Cal shares is very low. It's a great time to buy them."

"Never better, y'all. Never better," Stiche added, doing his bobble-head nod.

"My figures show we need more to buy Cal than the CACA cash we still have on hand, so we'll borrow that from the bank," Babcock went on.

"Thereby taking advantage of low interest rates," Stiche interrupted. "Everything's working in our favor!"

"I think this is the worst plan I've ever heard, Mr. Stiche, especially at this time," Regina said, focusing her grim gaze on Babcock.

"I appreciate your point of view. I have reservations too, Regina. However, it's already decided. We need to build our competitive advantage."

"I thought we were talking about a merger. What happened to that?" Leo asked, putting aside his half-consumed Strawberry Puff, his second for the day.

"They aren't interested," Babcock replied. "Either we buy them outright, or…"

"Or what?"

Babcock shrugged.

"Their equipment is outdated. They're in the same shape we were in before we bought the 500 series," Max Nussbaum said.

"But they have 500s," Stiche disputed.

"They have one production line they use for Big Nuts."

"We have excess capacity now; we'll move the rest of their production to our new machines," Babcock said. "How much will we get for their equipment, plus our old 100s?"

"I've got it listed for half a million, which is cheap. There are no takers so far," Max Nussbaum replied.

"Give it two more weeks and put it on eBay," Babcock said.

"An excellent idea," Stiche said. "If there are no more questions, I'd like to move on to the next item on the agenda. Some employees have been monopolizing the coffee machine for personal blends. The last time I had a cup of French Aroma someone had mixed in cocoa. That's your area, Regina."

"I think someone used caffeine-free coffee yesterday. I kept nodding off all day," Max Nussbaum added.

"It doesn't make any sense to buy Cal Foods. What happens when word gets out and the price increases?"

"Word better not get out, Regina," Babcock snarled as if he already blamed her for a leak that had yet to happen.

"I resent that!"

"About this coffee machine problem, I think we should post a sign where everyone can see it. Are there any other ideas?" Stiche interjected.

"It's symptomatic of employee discontent. I recommend we buy a coffee machine that can do different blends," Regina said, and waited for Babcock to object.

Pook doodled on her note pad, a cartoon of Babcock being kicked out Dough Inc.'s neo-classical front door. It was a high-heel shoe doing the kicking. She didn't look up until the discussion migrated to new products.

"Even though it's not a proper focus group, we've had some excellent feedback," she began. "I've developed a rating for each of our products based on number consumed and the kids' comments. Without a doubt our most popular donut is the Strawberry Puff."

"That's a surprise," Babcock sneered.

"SPs rate at 100. Choc Puffs are second at 85, followed by Pomegranate Dessert at 82. Our Doggy Donuts are at fourth place with 77."

"What?" Babcock demanded.

"Kids like the meat taste, Thomas, especially at lunch. I have their comments somewhere in here." Pook turned pages of her file. "'They're nummy in your tummy.' Your Rocklan said that."

"He'll be a marketing genius if he doesn't play professional football," Babcock gloated.

"Here's a good one. 'I woof them down.' Leo's daughter, Olivia, said we should call them K-9-4-Kids. Not as cute as Doggy Donuts, though I think it differentiates the product very nicely."

Babcock frowned. "What I don't understand is why there are two groups in the Dough team?"

Pook wasn't flustered. She'd practiced her answer for an hour and ten minutes.

"The groups are testing donuts, ours and the competition. This is the first focus group I've run since I started at Dough; there are a lot of donuts to evaluate. Ten people are plenty for a focus group."

Then, she busily studied her notes and waited for Babcock's comeback.

"Do you have any other doggy donut feedback, Eleanor?" Stiche asked.

Pook hurriedly turned pages. "Here's one. 'Now I see why my dog loves them,' and 'better than a hamburger because there's no lettuce.' Regina's daughter Claire said the last one."

"I hope she didn't eat too many," Regina said.

"It says three on the sheet. We ran out," Pook explained.

"How many calories in a Doggy Donut?" Stiche asked.

"I don't know. They don't test foods that aren't for human consumption." Pook returned to her summary sheet. "After Doggy Donuts, it's a 3-way tie with Thomas' Lemonettes , Jeremy's Chocolate Extreme, and our prototype kid donuts. One boy ate a dozen Lemonettes to get that score by the way."

"The Lemonette boy wouldn't be Rocklan, by any chance?" Regina asked sweetly.

Pook glanced at Babcock and kept her mouth shut. "Most of Jeremy's kid donuts have the same comment; 'too sweet,' so we're going to make a new batch and retest them tomorrow."

Babcock glanced at Max Nussbaum and winked.

Chapter 20.

"It's win, win, and win. The media's eating out of our hand, Stan," Forest bragged. "Three networks are doing an evening special on Fry's summer camp. Talk about stacking the election deck in our favor, and we don't have to pay for it."

"Governor Tubman?" Julian chimed in.

Governor Stanley B. Tubman jerked up his head. "What about Fry?"

"You might've dozed off, Stan." Forest hid his smirk in his meeting notes. "I was just saying the national networks will be there next week."

"All of them? Those people too? How did that happen?"

"I couldn't not invite them," Forest explained. "It'd look like we have something to hide."

Tubman heaved a sigh like a hippopotamus on a hot day. "Make a note; just invite our friends next time. Anything else?"

"The Treasurer's monthly report, Sir," Julian said, waving a wad of pages.

"Good news, I hope?"

"Tax receipts for July are down. Outgoing payments are up. That's not including WASP. We moved that to a direct charge against CACA revenue."

"Wasp?"

"The Weight Assistance and Support Plan, Sir. The deficit is way up compared to what you promised in your last speech. If you add in the WASP shortfall, it's worse than May."

"That's too much to keep straight! What's the bottom line?"

"We're in the hole again, Sir."

"But not as bad as we thought, right?" Tubman said, nodding hopefully.

"Actually, it's worse. You told the Legislature that July's deficit wouldn't top $45 billion, Sir."

"That was spur of the moment; I had to say something. Besides, wasn't it you who called CACA a cash cow?"

'And you said it'll be a frigging herd,' Julian thought. Instead, he smiled brightly. "They told us in school it always takes a few months for the revenue to stabilize with a new tax."

Forest snorted. He had more important matters to discuss. "About the media, Stan, we need to get your ducks in a row. You don't want to go off half-cocked, not with them there. It'd be worse than a fox in the hen house."

"Governor, it's still my turn," Julian said, frowning at Forest.

"I'm not in the mood for bad news," Tubman grumped.

"Then, I have some good news, Sir," Julian said, even more cheerful. "Chez Gerald has a new menu."

"About time! Is it any good?"

"I had dinner there last night, Sir. They do a very nice, rum-flambéed duck breast in burgundy sauce. And the flan was out of this world."

"We'll finish the budget tomorrow, Julian. Get me a reservation for lunch." Tubman turned to his fraternity brother as Julian hurried out. "Feel like some parlez vous francais for lunch?"

"Oui, oui," Forest replied just as breezily.

"What's on the Public Relations agenda for today, Hank?"

"I received a letter from one of our incubator companies earlier this week. Apparently, he just got another Green Alternatives Support grant to make propane from algae. He's risking life and limb to save the planet, and his neighbor's trying to get an injunction. Pond crud stinks, and it spoils the fishing, or some such nonsense. I've drafted up 358 pages of legislation for the Legislature to approve. Giving top priority to green initiatives will stop this anti-green crap in its tracks."

"We'll talk over lunch, and the Department of Agriculture can pick up the tab," Tubman said, mimicking a sly wink.

"Julian's got a point about this deficit thing, Stan. People are pissed."

"I've told him to spread the wealth around. I'm signing a contract with Cal Foods tomorrow for the school lunch program, the kids who aren't on the diet. They've got a nice little taco with refried beans they make somewhere in Mexico. I'm killing three birds with one stone. We're buying in bulk at 23 cents a serving."

"What's the third bird?"

"I'm taking Fry to Casa de Grande Avocados after the signing tomorrow," Tubman winked. "Vegetarian Tex-Mex with Ms. Nosey is a small price to pay to keep my mother off my back."

Forest quickly segued. "I'm still getting a couple of hundred letters a day from constituents, Stan. There's not a good one among them."

"They're all bad?"

Forest hauled a handful of papers from his hip pocket. He'd highlighted most in bright yellow, some in purple, a few in green.

"These are today's. 'Balance the budget or get out!'" he read. "'Try spending our money as if you'd worked for it!' All the yellows are like that."

"Not so bad. Give me a purple one,"

Forest looked down. "'Waste my money and I'll waste you!!'"

"That's not very nice. Don't they know it's the Legislature that causes deficits? I can't balance the budget without higher taxes."

"All these fiscal calamities are hurting our ratings, Stan. If the election was tomorrow, we'd be out on our asses."

"Julian assures me CACA money will start rolling in any day now. We'll have a nice little surplus come November if the Legislature doesn't waste it on building bridges."

"The good news is people forget in a month."

Tubman had perfected his yawn during six years of college. "What else?"

"I've had a ton of positive feedback on WASP," Forest replied. "Your Weight Assistance and Support Plan."

"I know what WASP is."

"Fifty-two percent of voters like it. The only complaint is we didn't include beverages on it."

"Fat people can't afford pop?"

"That's available on food stamps, Stan. Beer isn't."

Tubman's belly wobbled. "So put beer on WASP. The Constitution demands action when it's right for the masses. Health, safety, and welfare, and all that!"

"Lo-cal beer will guarantee the college student vote. If we include wine, it'll guarantee their professors too. If ever there was a time for executive action…"

"I'm on top of it, Hank. If anyone asks, say it's for medicinal purposes—red wine is good for you, right? Just make sure we give preference to local brews. I'm not supporting the German economy. That goes for the Frenchies too."

Chapter 21.

After leading Team Carbo to two humiliating losses in that morning's game of basketball, Rocklan Babcock wasn't in the mood for socializing; however, with a dirt bike at stake, he joined the other Dough Inc. kids in the miniscule patch of shade behind the Healthy Choices Summer Camp office.

"Babcock's destroying Dough," burned his ears before anyone noticed him.

Everyone shut up as he swaggered over. Once again, Frodo sat next to Jeffrey McTavish. Claire held her daily 'Hollywood' fan club meeting with two other girls, Racine Nussbaum and Olivia Frank, all three holding their breath until Rocklan decided where he'd sit down—he took the only seat left, opposite Jeffrey.

"You guys have weird donuts again," Rocklan observed, looking around. He took his first bite on a next-generation, new-and-improved Choc Puff, his third of the day.

"Mine's a different shape. No big deal," Jeff said quickly.

"What it's called? Wiener nut?" Rocklan guffawed, spitting bits of Choc Nut.

"It doesn't have a name yet. Frodo's mom is still working on it."

Jeff's father called the neo-éclair, '319.' A '3' was gooey chocolate-tofu, bran and corn flour mixed with oatmeal, like an under-baked brownie beneath a crisp outer layer. Shaped like a torpedo so it could be pushed into the mouth, it tasted great. Inside, Jeremy inserted a dollop of chocolate-fudge-tofu, aka '1'. However, '9' was a game changer; 'Chocolate Sin' was one of Jeffrey's favorite toppings. Altogether, the '319' was a gastronomic extravaganza, and very low calorie. Only steamed asparagus and boiled cauliflower without butter were lower.

"What's inside Frodo's?" Claire demanded, abandoning her adoring preteen coterie for Hollywood worship. She leaned across the trestle table and almost turned it over.

"It tastes like banana-crème pudding," Frodo squeaked from Jeff's side, licking his lips.

"It looks like poop."

Frodo replied with a shrug. From the outside, his '558' resembled a radioactive meteorite, a wrinkled lump of dark-brown rock with sparkly crystals. It looked like something a gnome might eat, or a cow had left behind.

"No one who's sane eats donuts with banana in them," Rocklan sneered.

"They're really, really good."

Frodo grinned for good reason. Before he went to summer camp, he preferred Choc Puffs over everything edible, including Big Nuts. He'd gorged on dozens of them, but never again. They simply couldn't compare to what he was eating. The 'banana' taste wasn't just flavoring; it was real, made by mashing tofu with bananas, the soft black and yellow ones that supermarkets couldn't sell. 'Banana-fu' was both cheap and good for you, with 20 percent of the calories of regular bananas.

Rocklan poked a hole in his donut and squeezed out a big pale custard glob that he promptly licked off, smearing his chin in the process.

"Choc Puffs are yummy! That's our new slogan; and I came up with it!"

Frodo forced another chunk into his wide-open mouth, crunching off chips from the hard outer layer and oozing yellow cream through his lips. "They're really, really chewy."

"Dog nuts are chewy," Rocklan said, utterly disgusted that anyone would put *that* in their mouth.

"It's the protein," Jeff said before he could stop himself.

He gnawed into his '319,' savoring choco-tofu and a hint of vanilla—which was his main contribution.

Ignoring his father's advice about always pursuing comments that didn't make any sense, Rocklan blurted out, "What do you guys think about Dough going public next week?"

"My mom's dead against it," Frodo said without thinking. "And Mr. McTavish thinks it's a disaster."

Jeff glared at his new best friend. "I don't know what he thinks. We don't talk about work."

"I heard him talking with my mom, yesterday" Frodo went on, despite five lectures from his mother about loose lips sinking ships. "He's really pissed."

"It wouldn't even be on the table except Mr. Stiche is sick," Jeff said.

"Mr. Stiche is a moron," Claire broke in.

"I bet Frodo's mom talks about Stiche all the time, same as my dad," Rocklan prompted, wishing he had his father's voice recorder.

"Mostly, she says Mr. Stiche is fat because he always samples donuts when he visits the production line."

"Actually, that would be Jelly-Belly McTavish," Rocklan laughed. "And Jeffrey is Jelly-Belly Junior."

Jeff thought it best to pretend he hadn't heard. He took a bite of '319' and masticated loudly.

"My mom says Dough's borrowing *waaay* too much money," Claire expounded, sounding exactly like her mother. "The last thing Dough should be doing is buying another company."

"My dad's doing what's best for the company," Rocklan fired back.

"My granddad says it's all the government's fault because of the fat tax," Racine Nussbaum interrupted.

"My dad says Dough needs to man up and move to Mexico," Olivia Frank snapped.

Claire flushed, sweaty and pink. "My teacher says taxes are only for our own good. Everyone needs to do their share, and share what they have with the less fortunate."

"It looks like we're doing basket weaving next," someone said as Team Carbo's med-student-assistant dumped an armful of multi-color wicker cane on the table.

"I can't wait," Rocklan grumped, staring at the other kids and thinking, 'red Yamaha 125 dirt bike.'

"Anyone for basketball?" Frodo asked brightly.

"You were lucky, that's all," Rocklan declared.

Frodo had scored Team Carbo's only point against Team Vitamin, and basketball wasn't his strong suit.

"It was skill."

"Like you'd know, McTavish. You give new meaning to chubby," Rocklan said.

Before summer vacation, Jeff rated 145.328 on his school's Fat Density Quotient. The school nurse thought it meant he was

45.328 percent overweight, which qualified him for a mandatory diet when school resumed in the fall.

Jeffrey McTavish was big for his age, chubby in the mid-section, too slow-moving to play any game except tug-o-war, and embarrassingly clumsy the rest of the time. However, he was strong enough to carry the trash can and both recycling bins out to the curb at the same time.

Before Jeff could say anything, the end-of-snack-time hooter honked three times.

Rocklan picked up his remaining Choc Nut and stood, stretching his tight iridescent T-shirt to show off his six-pack belly. "I'm sitting this one out. Anyone else not into basket weaving?"

Frodo grabbed a '269' and jumped up. The '6' was tasty orange sauce; it made him more energetic, and frisky. He looked taller standing up, still wiry alongside Rocklan, just not as skinny as he'd been when summer camp started. He made a beeline for the restroom, already squeezing and sucking at the side of the donut.

Jeff stood too, wondering whether his father's Saucy Passion filling affected Frodo the same way it affected him.

"You losing weight or something?" Rocklan sneered.

Jeff's summer shorts sagged. He hauled them up and tightened the cord.

Claire gazed across the table. "Rocklan, could you help me with my basket? My fingers aren't as strong as yours."

Chapter 22.

"Y'all, could I have you attention? Hush please! I'd like to get started."

Loudspeakers squealed feedback, grating like chalk on a blackboard as a sickly Herman Stiche adjusted his microphone. He stood center stage, on the highest platform festooned with July 4th bunting and Dough Inc's corporate flag, a big rainbow donut on a black rectangle.

"Isn't this exciting? Everyone gathered together to discuss the future of the company. It's just like a family getting together at Thanksgiving dinner."

He beamed at Dough Inc.'s employees. Of course, not everyone was there—he'd had to furlough some veteran employees; which Babcock blamed on decreased sales. The entire second shift had been cancelled for the very same reason; and it was right before noon, so a lot of people had gone to appointments on lunch break.

"Have I ever told y'all why my great grandfather put the first hole in a donut?" he began brightly.

"To get it to fry evenly," someone called from the ranks.

"The funny version," Stiche added seriously, craning his neck to see heads in the rear.

"At last year's Donut Day party; and it wasn't funny," a man shouted from the rear.

"Oh! Well, on to business then. Now, as y'all know, we installed the last of the 500 series machines this morning, so the first thing I need to do is..."

Stiche turned with a flourish. Behind him stretched a row of gleaming stainless steel machines and bright-yellow robots covered in plastic skins. He flipped the master switch and the machines came to life, red-warning lights flashing, alarm bells ringing shrilly, computer monitors showing production quotas and instantaneous quantities. Then, the conveyer belt clanked and began to move. Within seconds, donuts emerged from the fryers and advanced in a greasy line. Robotic arms hovered above, rearranging them for cream squirters and confectionary-sugar-shakers. At the end of the line, more robots picked up donuts, inspecting them in mid-air before dropping their claws to place them on packaging trays. Another robot dispatched four trays at a time on an overhead track to trucks waiting at the loading dock.

"Incredible, isn't it?" Stiche said in awe. "This is competitive advantage in the industrial age."

He adjusted the speed control to its maximum setting— 6,000 donuts a minute. Every second, a hundred donuts streamed down the production line, robot limbs moving at mind-boggling speed, so fast they were nearly invisible.

"Two million donuts yesterday and not a single reject all day. Of course, Dough had to automate eventually. It's the only way to keep down costs. I'd like to hear a big round of applause for Max Nussbaum who supervised the installation with his usual due diligence," Stiche continued.

"Thanks Max! I'm unemployed now," someone shouted.

"I'm sure y'all appreciate as much as I do that Max has agreed to postpone his retirement until the bugs are out. Thanks Max."

Stiche clapped much louder than everyone else combined.

"Of course, I'd be remiss if I didn't mention our Senior VP, Tom Babcock, who made all this happen." Stiche waved for Babcock to join him.

Faking humility, Babcock slowly ascended the stairs, waving to anonymous faces he didn't much care for.

"Y'all probably don't know that Tom's been very busy developing a plan to buy our biggest competitor. If you can't beat 'em, buy 'em out, I say."

Stiche waited for laughter; however, there was only a giggle from a teenage girl who was next to her boyfriend.

"As I was saying, our Senior VP's been burning the candle at both ends. Buying Cal Foods is a big step in our global strategy. Early next year, Dough will break ground for factories in Mexico and China. Now, the big news, that's capital 'B' Big news is... We're going public this Friday." Stiche waited again. "I'm sure y'all have lots of questions; however, let me just say this first. An opportunity like this comes along once in a lifetime. This is your chance to own a piece of the company. What I'd like y'all to do is buy Dough shares. I'm told they'll be trading under 'nut,' that's 'N-U-T.' We're going to post the share price right there so you can watch it go up."

Stiche pointed his middle finger at a huge overhead monitor displaying 'NUT $1.99.'

"For the same price as our regular donut, you can buy one share." He waggled the finger. "Buy one share every workday and you're on the way to being as rich as I am. Buy two and you'll be rich in half the time. That's how fortunes are made..."

"Is it true you're retiring, Mr. Stiche?" someone shouted from the right.

"I am not retiring; however, I do have an announcement to make."

Stiche paused to survey his audience. Center and rear were Dough Inc.'s factory workers in their regulation-logo-enhanced, red, yellow, or orange overalls, color according to rank. The warehouse crew in green filled in the sides, with purple maintenance clumped like grease in the middle. Quality control inspectors wore pristine white. Office staff, uniformly grey, stood in lonely unison at the front.

"The next few years will be a crucial period for the company. We stand on the threshold of an exciting new future, at a time when it's difficult to forecast what will happen. After a great deal of thought, I've decided to restructure senior management, effective immediately."

"Get rid of Babcock," a voice called from the rear.

"Mr. Babcock is President, starting today. As Chairman of the Board, I'll still be overseeing things from a distance, mostly concentrating on strategic planning and innovation. I'm all about fresh new ideas, as I'm sure y'all know. The day-to-day decisions will be up to Tom."

He stopped to clear his throat. Only a few people looked at him; the rest had their heads down.

"Now, as to the other changes we're making. I'm promoting Leo Frank to Senior VP, effective immediately. Eleanor Pook will become VP of Marketing on a permanent basis. I'm splitting Public Relations and Personnel, to take the stress off Regina King, who's been holding down both roles, and I must say, doing an excellent job with both of them. Ms. Wick will be our Acting Director of Personnel, under Tom's supervision, of course. That means we have another woman on the executive team; which is always great news. The lovely Petunia will be my personal secretary."

"You earned it, Petunia!" someone shouted from the rear.

"And because we're opening factories in Mexico and China, there's a new position, VP of Global Operations. Tom will fill it until we hire someone."

"This is crap," Regina muttered, barely containing herself. It was the first she'd heard of it.

"What about Jeremy?" a voice called from the right side.

"Mr. McTavish ought to be running the company!"

"Jeremy has his hands full with new product development," Stiche mumbled. "That's a very important job; and as we all know, he's exceptionally good at it. It wouldn't be wise to distract him with administration."

"You ought to make him Senior VP!"

"I'm sure everyone has lots of questions. The reorganization begins at the top and goes all the way down to the factory floor. I'd like Tom to talk about what this all means for you."

Babcock was the only executive in a three-piece suit. He cleared his throat.

"Thank you Mr. Stiche. First, let me say how pleased I am to be here at such an exciting time in Dough's history. As everyone knows, these are difficult times, what with all the new government regulations and competition. We all know about Big Nuts cleaning our fryers! After today, we're a different company. We'll still be a family; however, we'll be a faster, more flexible family, and entirely focused on our customers."

"Phooey!" someone shouted.

"There will be changes, of course, but life is full of changes. Some things might be hard to get used to; however, I know we'll all look back a while from now and ask ourselves, 'why didn't we always do things this way?'"

"Get to the point, Babcock!"

"With automation, we have to adjust our numbers," Babcock said, staring at the older employees gathered along the back wall and thinking they should've been fired and escorted from the building before the meeting.

"How many of us are going to get fired, Babcock?"

"I haven't decided," Babcock said calmly.

"I heard 30 percent!" a woman shouted.

"The good news is that after consolidation, all employees will get a share of the company."

"How big a share?" another voice demanded from the crowd.

"I haven't decided, but it'll be rather substantial for anyone who's worked here for ten years or more."

"What does 'substantial' mean?"

"You'll know when I decide," Babcock said, fixing his gaze on a pretty young woman in the third row from the back. He needed a personal secretary too.

'Heard it before."

"For those leaving, there'll be two choices. You can continue in the Dough family and work for commission, selling donuts in our exciting new door-to-door program; or work from home and sell over the Internet. Social media is the way of the future. Otherwise, you can take our very generous severance pay package."

"How much is generous?"

"A thousand dollars for every year you've been with the company, paid in monthly installments."

"With interest?"

"This is bullshit!"

"Over how many months?"

"That's crap and you know it, Babcock!"

"A lousy $15,000 after I gave this company the best years of my life!"

Babcock confronted the last one. "Donny, isn't it?

"It's Lonnie!"

"Think what you can do with all that money, Ronnie. You could buy a camper and travel."

"Not much of a camper for 15 grand."

"Okay, so you can add onto your house. A crafts room perhaps so you can take up leatherwork, or make model ships."

"I have carpal tunnel syndrome, Babcock."

"So splurge and go to the Bahamas. If I was you, I'd go to college. Factories are leaving this country for a reason," Babcock said, getting red in the face.

"Hey, Mr. Babcock?" a man called out.

Babcock searched for a familiar face in the unhappy crowd. "Yes?"

"Your robots is messin' up the donut trays."

Mangled donuts filled every tray. It was the grand finale of a back-up that went all the way to the fryers, which were beginning to smoke from over-fried dough. Custard-filled Choc Puffs piled up before and after the cream injectors, a great wall of them covered in cream, spilling onto the floor. Robots picked up the donuts that managed to find a way through on the conveyor belt, their two-talon claws squirting cream and custard everywhere. And even the expensive robotic scanner Dough Inc. purchased for final quality control misbehaved, rating every deformed donut as perfect.

Chapter 24.

"Governor Tubman, I'm Jordan Ryder. I wonder if you have a few minutes for an interview?"

"I'm sorry. I only do interviews if they're arranged through my press secretary. I'm sure you understand," Governor Stanley B. Tubman said, glancing at his watch and looking around for Julian and Forest. They'd disappeared the instant he plunged into a pool of media piranha.

"It won't take more than two minutes, Governor. Our viewers love to see you with kids, especially with an election coming up. This is a perfect setting for some great P-R on your summer camp program."

Ryder waved where Healthy Choices summer campers were finishing the morning's craft activity, building shelters for stray dogs and cats from recycled drink bottles.

Tubman frowned, mindful that sticking bottles together was more photogenic than face-painting. "I have time for five questions."

Ryder was a tall skinny man who had to stoop to stick his microphone in front of the Governor's face. While the video-photographer repositioned to get busy campers in the foreground, Ryder primped his dark-dyed hair to get the rugged masculine look that women adored. With a nod, his cameraman zoomed in for the Governor's head-and-shoulders close-up, adjusting his focus settings to see the Healthy Choices flag fluttering in the background.

"On three. One. Two..." At 'three,' the cameraman started filming

Ryder cleared his throat. "Jordon Ryder with news from our community. I'm here at Healthy Choices Summer Camp with Governor Tubman. Governor, people are worried about the deficit. Won't your free WASP meals make it worse?"

Vowing revenge, the Governor smiled into the camera. "Well, as you know Jordan, WASP stands for Weight Assistance and Support Plan. It's my administration's goal to assist people to lose weight and support healthy lifestyles."

"Doesn't WASP go out of its way to include trendy diets, Governor? I heard it covers that Surf and Turf diet where you eat lobster and filet mignon for every meal?"

"The legislation is very specific for just that reason, Jordan. A trained medical practitioner must recommend a diet to the Healthy Choices tribunal for it to be approved."

"Governor, once they approve a diet, is it true that WASP provides 100 percent of the cost, regardless of whether people actually lose weight?"

"I don't think we should deny people affordable healthy food because they're overweight, do you?"

"They wouldn't be overweight if they ate less food."

"You're not being fair, Jordan. What about people with eating problems, or hormone imbalances, that sort of thing, or people who are just big-boned and can't help it?"

"Do you think they should be eating lobster and steak at taxpayer expense, Governor? Wouldn't tilapia and lean hamburger be more reasonable?"

"I agree on principle, Jordan; however, people have allergies. They need special foods."

"Aren't you avoiding the issue, Governor? Everyone knows that trendy diets are very expensive."

156

"Svelte Melts are trendy and they cost $10. That's seems a lot for a sandwich; however, it's the same as a hamburger in a restaurant."

"A basic Svelte Melt is two pieces of low-cal bread and a slice of Swiss cheese, Governor. Is that a good way to spend taxpayers' money?"

"There are always tradeoffs, Jordan. We have to take a long term perspective when we're talking about the public good. It isn't about costs and benefits."

"Excuse me Governor; isn't that the argument you made for the Fat Tax?"

"You're thinking short term, Jordan. Everyone knows the means justify the ends. Making decisions is all about costs and benefits. If we don't consider the long term, we wouldn't have schools or bridges. A new bridge costs tens of millions. It's a big investment and we don't get a benefit right away unless you had to drive miles out of your way."

"What about bridges to nowhere?"

"In those cases we don't get the investment back until the bridge is demolished; however, we've had the convenience of using it all that time. I don't know about you, but there are times when I just want to go for a drive. Think of it as the freedom to go where we want, to explore new places. I'd like to continue the conversation, Jordan. Unfortunately, I have to meet Doctor Fry, who organized this wonderful opportunity for our less fortunate children."

"Governor, thank you very much for taking time out of your hectic schedule today."

"As I always tell my staff, the public good is all I care about! That's why I'm here today at the Healthy Choices Summer Camp."

Tubman beamed and gave an inspired victory wave to an imaginary crowd behind the camera before he went looking for Forest. As interviews went, it was run of the mill; much better if he'd had some of the summer campers gathered around him. Voters like to see their politicians with kids, if not their own then someone else's.

"Jordan Ryder's a mean #%*@er," Tubman snarled when he caught up with Forest.

"Thin as a snake with dark brown hair? He's with Media Services Network. What did you tell him, Stan?" Forest demanded.

"He was all over WASP and the budget. I gave him five minutes of poli-twaddle, the usual I'm-concerned-about-people stuff," Tubman chuckled. "Where's Fry? She promised me lunch."

"You're in the right place. At least she didn't invite the media," Forest grumped, leading the way to the front of the Healthy Choices trailer.

The Crown Cuisine Catering Company had decorated the inside of the trailer to resemble a restaurant in the south of France, with empty wine bottles in cane caddies, abundant travel posters, and multiple baskets of plastic fruit, flowers, and herbs.

"She must be joking," Tubman muttered, catching a glimpse of a tubby chef in traditional garb hurrying to greet him.

"Bonjour Monsieur Governor Toobman. My name, it is Pierre, and I am pleased to welcome you. Today, I have cooked for you, the delicious Provençal cuisine."

He had a black moustache, not like the Governor's, one with character, like a burly 19th century boxer.

"Where is that?"

"Sil vous plait?"

Julian stuffed plastic herbs in a cane basket. "It's in the south of France, Sir."

"At our last meeting you admired French food, Governor," Fry explained, stepping around Forest.

"French, Italian, German; they're gourmet compared to American Not Mexican; nacho chips, salsa, refried beans, tasteless cheese, and overcooked meat; it all tastes the same."

"I don't know if you've met Herman Stiche," Fry continued, dragging him across the room.

"Herman's with Dough, Stan," Forest hastened to add before she did.

"I'm Dough Inc, until Friday. That's when we go public. Then, it's up to the Board of directors," Stiche joked.

"Business must be good," Tubman said, looking down his nose as Fry hastily made introductions.

"It's passable, what with the lousy economy and lazy, uneducated workers. We're having a difficult time adjusting to the new taxes; still we're better off than our competition," Stiche went on.

"Glad to hear it. It's a pleasure meeting you," Tubman said, turning to escape.

"Strategic planning saved us. Business is all about strengths, weakness, opportunities, and threats."

"I'm sure it is."

Forest backed away. "If you'll excuse me, Herman, I need to talk with someone."

"Well-managed companies like Dough will always survive," Stiche said. "Difficult times demand difficult decisions. And new ideas. That's what I'm good at. Coming up with ideas."

"Lucky you," Tubman agreed.

He was tempted to say he had to discuss an important matter of state with his assistant; however, Julian was in deep conversation with Pierre about appetizers. That left a handful of doctors; and they probably voted for the opposition.

"Unfortunately, we've had to let go fifty percent of our employees."

"That's too bad. I'm sure firing an employee isn't easy."

"I've never seen donuts sales this bad," Stiche continued. "The last few months are as bad as the Thirties, Governor."

"I don't know how people survive."

"They cut back to essentials. No donut and coffee on the way to work, or for morning tea."

"There's not enough money for the luxuries in life. My family has to stretch every dollar just to buy the basics," Fry said, not adding that she'd just traded her last year's BMW sedan for a new Mercedes sports car.

"It's not just the private sector," Tubman said, his stance defying contradiction. "The government has to get $1.30 out of every dollar we spend."

"It's a $1.50 for us," Stiche interrupted. "Sometimes it's as much as two dollars when we're buying equipment."

"You're lucky you don't have to campaign. Political contributions are the first things people cut back on."

"I'm sure it's serious," Fry said. "Governor, it looks like Pierre is ready to serve lunch."

They took their places at the south-of-France table, a crisp white tablecloth set with rustic hand-painted china plates and antiqued silverware, all made in China.

"This is your show, Doctor Fry. I insist you sit at the head," Tubman said, taking the chair to her right.

With Forest on his right, he thought he was safe from Stiche. Unfortunately, he sat opposite.

"Our first course is a nasturtium and goat cheese salad," Fry explained. "You can eat the flowers, by the way. They're a little bitter; very high in anti-oxidants, though."

"What are you eating, Herman?" Tubman asked. If there was dressing on his salad, he couldn't see it.

"I preordered. I'm on the Surf and Turf diet," Stiche said.

"They're generous portions," Tubman said enviously.

Stiche cut into a one-pound lobster tail, and stabbed a chunk with his fork. "Very tasty, I must say."

"With all that butter, it can't be good for you," Fry said pointedly.

"Surf and Turf puts quality ahead of quantity," Forest objected. "It's all about enjoying what you eat."

"Hank's wife's been on Shellfish and Caesar for nearly two years. She's bigger than ever," Tubman chuckled. "It got so expensive that he had to get the state to pay for it."

"The state's paying for my meals too," Stiche admitted, turning his attention to a fat filet mignon. He sliced it in two, still red inside, bloody juices spilling out. "Medium rare. M-mm-mmm." He closed his eyes and savored the taste. "I hate to admit it; this is better than a Strawberry Puff."

Fry could taste the blood dripping on Herman Stiche's plate. "What were you saying about fundraising, Governor?"

"Getting blood out of a stone would be easier. Politics is all about relationship building. Working together for the common good. Public-private partnerships strive for win-win teamwork."

"Back-scratching by any other name," Stiche remarked caustically. Only then, he scrutinized the Governor. He smiled slightly. "Being in business is no different. We do whatever it takes to survive," he added quietly.

"How's that lobster, Herman?" Tubman asked as if he hadn't heard.

"The best I've had, Stan. I like not paying for my meals."

Tubman laughed. "So you'll vote for me?"

"It'll take more than free lobster."

"What would it take?" Forest asked.

Stiche shrugged. "I'm open to offers."

Chapter 25.

"Run!" Rocklan Babcock screamed at the top of his lungs.

Jeffrey McTavish didn't run; he galloped—anything faster than walking wasn't his strong suit; however, once an elephant got momentum, nothing stopped it. And yet, as big as he was, he seemed to have springs on his feet. His legs were more powerful too, so he covered the ground faster than ever before. His gym shorts fluttered around his waist. His adult-XL *Healthy Choices Summer Camp* T-shirt flapped on his chest—it had been tight two weeks ago.

Rocklan gaped. "What the…"

Jeffrey was holding his own against the Team Vitamin kid. The Team Protein kid drew away at the turn, yet as they raced back to the start, Jeffrey very slowly made up lost ground. He blasted across the finish line still in second place, thrust the baton into Frodo's hand and collapsed onto the grass, gasping.

"Go Frodo," Jeremy wheezed.

A hobbit chased by ogres couldn't have run as fast as Frodo Pook. Jeremy wondered if low wind resistance gave Frodo an advantage over two long-legged 13-year-old boys from the other teams. Maybe gravity affected him differently; his feet barely touched the ground. It certainly wasn't muscles because Frodo was wiry; however, what he did have, he used to advantage. He was also agile. He pivoted around the halfway mark clearly in the lead, and widened the gap on the way back.

With an unbeatable head start, Claire lumbered off. She was wearing her mother's spinning shorts, and they were still tight.

"I'll make it up," Rocklan bragged as Team Carbo's lead shrank to nothing. "You can do it, Claire," he called feebly.

"Give it everything you've got, Sweetie-pie" Regina screamed from the spectator area on the other side of the field.

Claire came in second, shoved the baton into Rocklan's hand, tottered over to her backpack and slumped over it, digging in the side pocket for the Choc Puff she'd stored for emergencies.

It didn't please Herman Stiche that Team Carbohydrate finished last. He crossed the field to coach them for the last event, Tom Babcock striding beside him.

"The piggy back race is ours for the taking," Rocklan boasted. He rubbed his ankle as if still in agony from the morning basketball game, which hadn't gone well for Team Carbo. "I'll carry Frodo. Jeffrey's with Olivia. And Claire, you're carrying Racine."

"McTavish and Pook would be better," his father said.

The five-minute warning whistle interrupted him. Anyone could see why he was right to be worried. Team Vitamin's front runner was a mean bull of a boy with already hairy legs. A cruel-looking skin-head midget was mounted on his back, practicing charging their teammates, all girls. Team Protein was fielding all boys, more matched in size; however, they were scarred street fighters from the east side of town.

"Dad, it's my team!"

Babcock examined his son with a frown. "You're looking flabby."

Rocklan returned a half-hearted shrug. "I've been eating donuts for two weeks, Dad."

"You also haven't been doing your exercises at home."

"How would you know? You're never home."

"Team Carbo to the starting line," one of the med-student-assistants bellowed over the loudspeaker, interrupting the Healthy Choices theme song, stolen from 'Star Wars.'

"Frodo you're riding with me," Rocklan said, glaring and silently daring his father to make a fool of himself.

"McTavish carries Pook, and that's final, son!"

Stiche stepped between them, raising his voice the way he did when he made a strategic decision that no one agreed with. "This is my team, y'all. We're not here to eat donuts! Babcock Junior, undo your shoelace."

"It's not a three-legged race," Babcock Senior countered.

"Competitive advantage, Tom! Your son's job is to take down the big kid at the start when he doesn't expect it. Once he gets moving, we won't stop him." Stiche grasped Rocklan's shoulder, leaned in, and whispered, "When the race starts, stumble into him. Make sure you lose your shoe, but keep going. We don't want them saying we cheated."

"Right, Mr. Stiche. I got it, Sir!"

Stiche nodded approval. "McTavish and Pook, you're responsible for decimating any Proteins and Vitamins in range. That'll leave our girls a clear path to the finish. Got it?"

"Yes Sir," Team Carbohydrate echoed.

The very instant the hooter tooted, Rocklan stumbled sideways as if he'd tripped on his shoelace, dropping off Racine Nussbaum before he rammed into Team Vitamin's front runner. Both runner and rider went down hard, taking the next pair of Team Vitamin's girls with them. Jeff's start was also delayed when a Team Protein rider almost shoved Frodo off his back. Luckily, Frodo clung on with one arm around Jeff's neck and shoved with the other.

"Leggo," Jeff gagged as he struggled for air.

Halfway to the turning point Team Carbohydrate held third, fourth, and fifth places; however, Jeff was bearing down on second place Team Protein. As he drew alongside, the riders flailed at each other.

"It's donut time, Fat Boy," the Team Protein rider derided as Jeff veered away.

"You drool over Big Nuts!" Frodo shouted as Jeff swerved in.

The leggy runner tried to dodge, twisting his ankle even as his rider slid down to his butt, adding insult to injury. They slowed to a hobble as Jeff bolted after the leader.

Jeff and Frodo caught up at the turning point, a portable sign that read 'doctor's parking only.' Jeff barged into the leader a moment before he crashed into the sign. That left Team Carbohydrate's Claire and Olivia against a pair of Team Protein girls. Despite Olivia's iridescent-green T-shirt, the Team Protein rider easily recognized her from her latest commercial—she ice-skated and ate donuts at the very same time. Team Protein was so distracted by celebrity status, they crossed the finish line a nose-length behind the Team Carbo girls.

Chapter 26.

"Thirty nine cents!" Stiche exploded. "It was $1.16 an hour ago."

"It'll probably go lower, Herman," Babcock said slyly. "It takes a while for prices to settle down. Stock trading is all about having the right information."

Both Stiche and Babcock had their cell-phones out, both sending text messages to their stock brokers, one buying NUT, one selling NUT, both in very large quantities.

"How low?" Stiche demanded, close to panic as his fortune disappeared before his eyes.

An overhead monitor displayed NUT's current price, with relevant news items scrolling across the bottom. Max Nussbaum's most-trusted technician had bolted it to the Boardroom ceiling, directly above Herman's portrait to indicate which Stiche had taken the company public.

"In this market, it might get down to the book value of our assets. That's about 25 cents," Babcock replied, seeming unruffled and reading the Wall Street version of news.

The market reaction to Dough Inc.'s takeover offer for Cal Foods was exactly what Babcock expected. He responded with unsettling calm, buying shares of NUT, and selling his holdings in CAL as its price soared to $3.76.

Hurriedly, Stiche typed in another sell-NUT order. The rest of Dough Inc.'s executive team had taken their seats before the transaction executed. Selling 1,200,000 shares at 35 cents only made his mood worse.

"Let's focus on competitive advantage. Bring us up to date on new products," Stiche said, glaring at Jeremy, his first day back from vacation.

"I'll begin with a review of our focus group at Healthy Choices Summer Camp. It was very enlightening," Jeremy began.

He was in a good mood. He'd traded all of his NUT stock as soon as the market opened on Monday, selling all 150,000 shares at $1.83.Pook had waited an hour before she sold hers. Still, $1.51 was a lot better than 34 cents. Then, 33 cents flashed on the screen and Stiche looked very pale. He reached for his cake donut, his hand trembling.

"I'm sure it'll go up soon, Mr. Stiche," Pook said with stoic assurance. "After two weeks of testing our donuts with preteens, the results are: Jeremy's new and improved Choc Puffs are a clear winner, then Strawberry Puffs and Hug Nuts, followed by Chocolate Extreme dessert donuts and Doggy Donuts."

"What are Hug Nuts?" Jeremy said, looking more like a Ginger Monkey than ever.

"They're Huge Nuts, without the 'e'," Babcock replied, without giving details. "Thirty two cents! Who would've thought it'd go that low?"

"What are Huge Nuts without the 'e'?"

"HUG NUTS!" Babcock snarled.

Jeremy slowly looked around, comprehension dawning, his head aching on the right side. "You copied Big Nuts while I was on vacation, didn't you?"

"We couldn't wait until we bought Cal Foods. We had to do something," Stiche replied. "Our competitive advantage was being flushed down the toilet by inaction."

"My Hug Nuts are not a copy," Babcock cut in. "I added a sugar-glazed topping, and they're bigger!"

"That makes all the difference," Jeremy sneered.

"If you can't beat 'em, imitate 'em; and cut the price by ten percent," Leo muttered.

"We were losing market share. We had to match the competition," Stiche went on; not at all sure he'd made the right decision.

"We didn't need to match anything. We bought them," Jeremy retorted.

"Kids still like Puffs more," Pook pointed out. She'd been sworn to secrecy regarding ~~Huge~~ Hug Nuts.

"What else did we have in the summer camp tests?" Stiche inquired.

"I'd like to hear the results for my donuts for kids," Babcock asked directly.

"Lemonettes finished eleventh overall. We had a few reports of kids getting sick. Not food poisoning, fortunately. I think the icing must've soured in the heat," Pook said.

"We can fix that with preservatives," Babcock interrupted.

"It isn't just the icing," Pook continued, pulling pages from her pink-and-purple focus-group file. "The kids' comments are very revealing. 'I'm nauseous after one. After two, I puke my guts out,' 'Better than nothing,' 'Gross to the max.' The comments are all negative."

Babcock regarded her suspiciously. "They were in fifth place."

"That was before Hug Nuts. Everything changed after we sorted out the sweetness problem with Jeremy's kid donuts." Pook turned back to her focus-group file and left it at that.

"Give me the bottom-line, Pook?" Stiche said, not daring to look at the monitor after 32 cents.

"We should go all out on the new-and-improved Choc Puffs, Mr. Stiche. A full marketing blitz, in-store advertising, TV commercials, and penetration pricing. I'm thinking $1.80 each with a discount for three or more."

"I don't think we should give up on diet donuts," Jeremy said, looking around the table.

Except for Pook, there was no support. Even Regina rolled her eyes, and Max Nussbaum went so far as to shake his head.

"Jeremy, it would be a good idea if you didn't mention low-calorie donuts again. Throwing out red herrings just distracts everyone."

"Mr Stiche, I really think…"

"Enough with the diet donuts," Babcock said loudly, now fuming.

"If Jeremy's right, it's a completely untapped market," Pook muttered, her head down.

"If that's what Jeremy believes, he should quit and go into business for himself," Stiche grumbled, unable to stop himself from glancing at the monitor. Thirty one cents!

"I think we should go all out on Hug Nuts," Babcock said.

"They'll take market share from Big Nuts and waste shelf space. We need it for dessert donuts, and for Jeremy's kid donuts," Pook said meekly.

"After one lousy focus group you want to take his kid donuts to market?" Babcock demanded.

"You want new product or not, Thomas?" Regina muttered.

"This isn't a personnel matter, Regina!"

"I'm P-R now! It's not a financial matter either."

"That's enough! Thirty cents!" Stiche shoved back his chair. "The ship is sinking, and you're not manning the pumps like you're supposed to. I won't have mutiny on my ship! If you don't want to pump, get off!"

Stiche stormed out of the Boardroom leaving stunned silence in his wake. A full minute passed, the NUT price on monitor bouncing between 29 cents and 31 cents. Babcock calmly purchased another 1,200,000 shares before he smiled to himself.

"That was helpful," Leo said quietly.

Max Nussbaum chuckled. "I'm glad I'm retired."

"By the way, is there any news on the equipment sale?" Babcock asked.

"Everything sold on eBay this morning; $105,000."

Only then did Jeremy smile, looking right at Pook, who seemed quite surprised.

Chapter 27.

Some months later.

"You've seen the new donut billboard," Governor Stanley B. Tubman said even before he sat down.

The billboard was impossible to miss, a huge pile of appetizing donuts, 'Healthy American Donuts' on top, and a web address underneath. It was at Exit 3, where the traffic slowed down for the bridge, directly across from "Elect Suzie Manson; today's Governor for tomorrow's problems.' Everyone who saw the billboard said it looked as if plump Suzie Manson was salivating over which donut to eat next.

Doctor Fry glanced at her watch. "I thought I had the wrong day."

It was less confrontational than reminding the Governor that their lunch meeting was scheduled for 55 minutes earlier.

"Important matters of state will have to wait today," Tubman said, the aroma of fresh baked baguettes from the kitchen boosting his humor.

He'd been stuck in the sand on the 16th hole when Hank Forest called to say that his 'Elect Tubman' fund was officially bankrupt. His already bad mood became even worse. With a month remaining before the election, they had to move quickly to refill the coffers.

The Governor looked around Chez Donald before inhaling deeply. "M-m-m. There's nothing like..." He sniffed again. "... Food de France. Give me puffy little pastries with chocolate sauce any day. Speaking of pastries, what about those diet donuts, Francine? Bit of a shock, eh?"

"Going low cal is so creative. Not at all what you'd expect from a donut company," Julian added.

"I spent most of yesterday looking into their claims," Fry said in her usual sober way.

"Good choice for lunch, Francine," Tubman declared. Chez Donald wasn't his favorite restaurant for lunch; however, Healthy Choices was footing the bill so he wasn't about to object. "Why can't American restaurants decorate like this?"

The upstairs' salon was festooned in seasonal yellow and orange silk-screened leaves with bright red tablecloths. The same leafy pattern decorated the menu, along with red and yellow eddies. It looked as if someone's kid had been finger-painting. Unfortunately, it made the scroll of items and prices difficult to read.

"Can you see what that is?" he asked, squinting hard and stabbing his finger at elaborate swirls.

"Escargot, sir," Julian replied.

"I don't like snails. Never did. Frog legs are okay. They taste like my grandmother's pork-fried chicken legs. She used to dip them in oregano; or was it basil?"

"About the ads, Governor; the claims are rather extreme; however...."

"I spoke to the Attorney General this morning, Doctor Fry," Julian jumped in. "He'll press a false advertising charge if the Governor tells him to."

"I wouldn't rush to judgment. We analyzed 23 donuts in the hospital laboratory."

"Lavatory?" Tubman said, glancing up from the menu. "That doesn't sound very hygienic. You'd think a hospital would know better." A frown furrowed his forehead, his eyes red and watering, more from election stress than allergies. "Julian?" he pointed at his menu again.

"Pomme frites, Sir."

"So it is!" Tubman blinked rapidly and peered at the menu. "Awfully small print. There ought to be a law against it. What about your hospital lavatory?"

"All the tests came back with the same result," Fry said with a sour face.

Tubman held the menu inches from his face and scanned for his favorite. "Damn, they've changed the menu again! La spécialité de chef isn't Canard à la Donald! I don't want to eat Braised Boar with Artichoke on Friday!"

"And what was the result, Doctor?" Julian asked, suddenly suspicious.

Doctor Fry had called for an appointment at 9:15 am, before he'd even sat down with his start-the-morning-on-a-high-note blended coffee. He was surprised, although he'd seen the donut billboard on the way home the previous afternoon. The eleven pm news picked up the story. He wasn't at sure what all the fuss was about. It was very straightforward; some people ate donuts for two months, and lost weight.

"Overall, our results are better than the website claims," Fry said. "On average they have less than 20 percent of the calories of a regular donut, plus they're very high in anti-oxidants, vitamins, calcium, and iron. They have more protein than eight ounces of steak, without the fat."

"So this company, Healthy American Donut, is not out of line?" Julian pressed.

"One donut is better for you than four servings of your mother's steamed kale."

"Kale probably tastes better," Tubman grumped.

"They're delicious, Sir," Julian said. "I had a Flaky Farmhouse with my morning coffee. It's got little bits of crunchy oatmeal on top and caramel cream inside. It tasted better than a Big Nut; a lot better."

"That's what my daughter said last night. She ate half a Country Crisp and skipped dinner."

"I can't belief Chef Donald is not frying his duck. I mean…" Tubman tossed the menu on the table and threw up his hands. "He's famous for it."

"He's serving turkey instead, Sir," Julian said. "For Thanksgiving."

"Since when do the French celebrate Thanksgiving? They're socialists!"

Julian looked shocked. "I celebrate Bastille Day."

"Well, I don't!"

"They gave us the Statue of Liberty, Sir."

"Can we stay on topic?" Fry interrupted. She waited until the Governor ceased grumbling about 'canard.' "These diet donuts would fix the school lunch crisis."

"Crisis? What crisis?" Tubman asked.

"I sent you a report." Fry glared at Julian.

"Don't look at me. I put it in his in-tray."

"What report?" Tubman demanded.

"School diets aren't working out like we expected, Sir."

"Two out of three overweight kids are skipping lunch," Fry explained.

"There's a budget saver right there."

175

"Governor, they're bringing snacks from home, and the rest of the kids are eating their leftover meals."

"Your report said something about them not losing weight," Julian added, looking at Fry to confirm it.

"School FDQs are up 9.6 percent."

"Remind me, Doc; FDQs are…"

"It's your Fat Density Quotient hard at work educating the overweight masses, Governor."

Tubman glowered back at her. "And this is my fault because…."

"No one said it was your fault, Governor." Fry took a deep breath. "If we serve these new diet donuts for lunch, I can promise you the kids will eat them and they'll lose weight."

"Then, we'll look into shifting the contract to Dough Inc. Problem fixed. Can we order lunch now?"

"It's not Dough Inc. that makes them, Sir," Julian said.

"Healthy American Donut Company does, Governor. I had my staff look into it. It's registered to McTavish and Pook."

"Puke?"

"Sir, you met Ms. Pook at Healthy Choices Summer Camp," Julian explained. "She's one of Dough's VPs. The one who you said looked like an elf."

Tubman scratched his head. "Not Dough, but owned by Dough's employees? It sounds like corporate fraud to me."

Fry heaved a sigh. "They used to work for Dough, Governor. They quit and started their own company."

Chapter 28.

"What's for breakfast?" Babcock called, gleefully sliding his briefcase across the kitchen floor and sending the family dog careening for cover.

"Healthy American Donuts, Dad," Rocklan announced, digging into the platter in the center of the table.

"I can get donuts at work," Babcock grumped, his good mood evaporating before he sat down. "What happened to scrambled eggs and sausage, or hash browns and bacon? That's American as apple pie."

"They stopped serving that stuff in the 20th century. Too much cholesterol. Any more Elf Nuts, Mom?"

"Elf Nuts," Babcock repeated. "What are Elf Nuts?"

"Donuts for kids," Rocklan's gap-toothed, six-year-old sister, Madison, giggled. She held up hers. It had gnaw marks all over the sides.

Babcock peered at it. "What is it?"

"It's an Elf Nut, Daddy!"

"So you said."

"It's a donut, only it's good for you," Rocklan beamed. "You can lose weight by eating them."

"You need to lose weight. From now on, you exercise an hour a day, same as I do."

"They taste great, Daddy."

"It's hard as rock on the outside, but inside… Wow!" Rocklan said, pawing through the platter to find another.

Madison poked her tongue through the hole she'd made, and suctioned out creamy sauce. When she put it on her plate again, brown smears covered her face.

"It must be some sort of test market thing from my i-Team?" Babcock thought aloud.

The i-Team was Dough Inc.'s new 'innovate Team.' His mantra 'Innovate or Expire,' was much more up-to-date than Stiche's strategic planning. It fit right in with his visionary, globalized, automated, customer–centered, employee-focused, branded, highly responsive company.

"I'm glad you like it; however, I could do without the sound effects."

"Elf nuts are yummy, Daddy." Madison gurgled saliva and sauce and sucked even harder.

Babcock sat with his back to the kitchen, gazing across a yard covered with leaves, orange and gold stragglers fluttering down. A week after he'd taken control of the company, McTavish and Pook handed in their resignations. With them out of the way, he'd merged marketing and new product development, despite Stiche's protests. The protests stopped when Stiche saw the personnel savings.

He nudged Rocklan, who was delighted after discovering an untouched Elf Nut under an X-nut.

"Don't make plans for the weekend. You're raking the yard."

"What's wrong with the lawn mower?" Rocklan asked, as moody as his father when things didn't go his way.

"Sitting on your flabby butt isn't exercise."

Babcock picked up the X-nut, savoring the distinctive scent of passion fruit cream filling. On second thought it smelled tantalizingly fresh. His first bite was definitely invigorating. There was no boring hole in the center. Instead, tangy yellow-orange sauce bulged from inside. It was tasty like a cake donut on the outside, not greasy in the slightest, perfect for a busy executive's breakfast, or served à la Mode at an elaborate dinner party.

"Yours tastes as good as it looks?" he muttered, watching his wife slurp blueberry cream from a Protein Extreme.

Mirabelle nodded and gorged at the same time, her edgy palate relishing every delicious crumb. It was easily digested too, ideal for active upper-class mothers who spent two hours with a tennis coach after chauffeuring their children to school.

"Kids call them Elf Nuts, Daddy, 'cause they're for health," Madison said, burping loudly.

"Healthy donuts; how creative is that?" Babcock said, sipping his morning black coffee.

"On the website, it says an Elf Nut with a glass of milk contains 100 percent of your daily vitamins. It has anti-oxidants too," Rocklan said, busily excavating his Elf Nut. With the spongy dough interior just in sight, he sought creamy Nirvana, just a little bit farther.

"Anti-oxidants will add years to your football career, Rocky," Babcock said, his mood bubbling like champagne.

"I think I might have a double tennis session today," Mirabelle muttered, her heart already racing with anticipation.

Babcock couldn't help wondering if the 'X' in 'X-nut' stood for something other than X-generation. He'd gulped it down in a matter of seconds. Strangely, he hadn't felt this frisky since his wife went lingerie shopping at Vicky's Enigma five years ago.

His i-Team was definitely on top of things. They had new and improved donut products rolling out the door every day; Hug Nuts with ten percent more cream, multi-colored icing on cake donuts instead of the usual chocolate, caramel, and vanilla, new paper bags to carry six regular donuts at a time without them sticking together. Why not healthy donuts?

"Claire said Jeff's dad invented them?" Rocklan eyed the remaining X-nut, even though he was too full to finish his second Elf Nut.

"McTavish? Hardly! We fired him months ago."

"Claire said he went into business with Frodo's mom and bought all Dough's old equipment."

"Impossible! We sold it on Ebay months ago."

Chapter 29.

"I'm hearing stories about a new donut company," Babcock began.

"NUT's at 28 cents," Leo griped, red-faced, with little quivers at his temples.

It was so obvious who he blamed that Babcock kept his head down, all the way to his seat at the head of the table.

"It's ridiculous! We're worth far more than that." Trevor Fingledorp was previously VP of Cal Foods' Manufacturing. He came with the acquisition, an ex-Marine who'd seen service in Germany, the perfect person to head Global Operations.

"It'll be five dollars a share soon; now that I've got the 500s running properly," Max Nussbaum said, although he seldom agreed with his nemesis—his Manufacturing Department now reported to Global Operations.

"Obviously, the word hasn't gotten to Wall Street," Regina snapped, thinking she should've sold her shares three months ago.

Ms. Wick perked up. "So P-R's the problem?"

"Wall Street doesn't know anything about our donuts. We need a New York P-R firm."

"The market knows what the market knows," Sy Renard declared.

Renard was Dough Inc.'s new VP of Innovation, two years out of Harvard Business School, a whiz kid who'd started an Internet gaming company in his basement before he graduated from high school. He worked as a derivative-trader's assistant on Wall Street during his college summers, and wrote articles for in-flight magazines on how to be a brilliant entrepreneur in today's global markets.

"Buy on the way down, sell on the way up, that's my approach," Leo continued.

"Except the price is going the wrong way," Regina said.

"I gave my broker a factory tour. He was very impressed with our operations. He insists it's a short term adjustment," Max Nussbaum said.

"He's right about the adjustment part," Regina sniped again.

"Sales will improve. It's just a matter of time with all our new products," Renard said.

"I'm glad you had the foresight to buy Cal Foods. Between their Big Nuts and the school lunch contract, we'll be okay," Fingledorp said, with a grateful nod in Babcock's direction.

"I think we paid twice what they were worth; and we borrowed way too much," Regina cut in.

Renard glared at her. "Some of us need to be more supportive of executive decisions."

The boardroom babble didn't diminish until Babcock slammed his executive portfolio flat on the table. Everyone looked up.

"This morning I heard about a new donut company. It seems there are traitors from within."

"Someone's spying for the competition?" Leo inquired, following Babcock's gaze around the Boardroom.

"Two people," Babcock said, watching Regina, who stared straight back.

"Who?" Max Nussbaum asked.

"McTavish and Pook." He wrinkled his nose as if a plate of decaying shrimp was in front of him instead of a plate of sugared donuts fresh from the fully automated fryer.

"Jeremy? I don't believe it."

"Ms. Wick, your role in these meetings is to take minutes," Babcock snapped.

"But Mr. Babcock, you said I was head of Personnel."

"I said you will represent me when I can't attend meetings! You're not supposed to contribute your thoughts in Executive Meetings, just take notes." Babcock cleared his throat. "Regina, I was wondering whether you could shed some P-R light on the matter."

"What matter?"

"Pook and McTavish."

"I'm sure I know less than you do." Regina doodled wallpaper patterns on her notebook. "Pook called me last week to tell me they're selling donuts to El Gasso gas stations and Stark's coffee shops, that's all!"

"It definitely wasn't one of ours," Max Nussbaum muttered.

"Nussbaum, what are you going on about?" Babcock demanded.

"I got a donut at El Gasso when I filled up yesterday afternoon. It tasted a lot like Jeremy's dessert donuts. It was tasty and fresh. But the filling; now that was superb."

"They're a small local manufacturer. Nothing to worry about," Regina added quickly.

"What if I told you my wife bought their donuts at SuperDuper this morning?" Babcock interrupted.

"Our stock price is going down like the Titanic and you're worried about two ex-employees selling donuts in few lousy supermarkets?" Regina said.

"That's it! I'm selling out!" someone shouted in the hall.

Babcock stared at the monitor; everyone did. 'NUT 0.19' had no explanation for nearly a minute. Then, the news-line scrolled, 'Wall Street trader expects Dough Inc.'s sales down 33 percent next quarter. Investors abandon ship.'

"@%&#ing idiot!" he spluttered.

"Would you like some coffee and a fresh cake donut, Mr. Babcock?"

Babcock got out his cell phone and punched speed dial for his stock broker. Then, he couldn't decide whether he should buy or sell, so he stared at it.

"Coffee and donut, Mr. Babcock?" Ms. Wick asked again.

"No!"

"There's no need to shout at the elderly. I'm sure Ms. Wick can hear as well as I do."

Babcock inhaled three times before he finally breathed out. "Thank you, Max. By the way, do you happen to know who bought our old equipment on Ebay?"

"You said it didn't matter unless it was Cal Foods," Max Nussbaum replied haughtily.

"I know what I said!"

"We ought to do some of Stiche's strategery stuff and figure out what to do next," Leo grumped, his retirement fund vanishing before his eyes.

"Strategy!" Babcock growled.

"We're strategerizing, aren't we?"

"While we still can," Regina muttered.

"We should've listened when McTavish tried to sell us on healthy donuts," Leo lamented.

"What's that supposed to mean?" Babcock demanded.

"My husband tried a healthy donut on Monday."

"And your point, Regina?"

"All he's talked about is how good they taste. He's eaten their donuts every day this week and he's lost three pounds."

"I find that hard to believe," Babcock said.

"Claire's eating them at school as part of an experiment. She already looks thinner."

"I ate two Elf Nuts yesterday and my bowel movements have been much easier," Max Nussbaum said.

"Suggestions, anyone?" Babcock said, gritting his teeth.

"Buy them out before they have a chance to expand," Sy Renard said.

"Knowing McTavish, that won't happen," Babcock replied. "We'll have to cut our prices and force them out of business."

"Sue them for stealing company secrets. We used to shoot spies in the Marines."

Regina glared at Fingledorp. "Jeremy McTavish didn't steal anything. Pook told me he developed his donuts at home."

"Whose team are you on, Regina?"

She turned her glare on Babcock. "We ought to be developing healthy donuts of our own."

"The i-Team's already looking into it," Babcock said with a sly smile at Sy Renard.

Chapter 30.

"These dessert donuts are really quite good aren't they?" Governor Stanley B. Tubman said, looking down. An empty plate stared back at him, just a smear in the center.

"Much better than the donuts we had last time," Forest agreed. He scooped cream with a spoon and held it out. "This tastes a bit strange, though."

Fry gave it a cursory glance. "It's probably calorific acid. Restaurants are using it to hide fat calories so they don't pay a higher tax rate. The calories are still there, just harder to measure."

"Is that even legal?" Forest asked, licking the spoon.

He sucked in his bloated cheeks as if calorific acid was already eroding the inside of his mouth. Instead, the cream tasted refreshingly tangy, not like artificial cream made from corn syrup.

"It is until you pass a law to stop it. There was probably 1,000 calories on your plate. I guarantee it tested at half of that," Fry continued. "Everyone's cheating, including companies making healthy food. My lab's even found calorific acid in baby food."

"That'll take care of the fat baby problem," Tubman chuckled.

"Actually, I'm certain the new company made these donuts," Fry said.

"The one claiming their donuts have a third of the calories?" Julian asked. He turned over the remains of his donut, inspecting the bottom.

"It's closer to a quarter, actually," Fry said. She'd chosen low-fat frozen lime yogurt for her dessert, and regretted it.

"They don't taste low calorie," Tubman said, still savoring his last bite. "The filling is orange, not red like it usually is."

"It's Passion fruit, Sir," Julian whispered. "My friends say it's a natural aphrodisiac."

"A donut that makes you feel sexy; seriously?" Tubman whispered back. The idea tantalized him as much as the residue on his palate. It made his heart surge. "Whatever will they think of next?"

"You're telling me I could lose weight eating this?" Forest joked, greedily slurping thick Chocolate Sin sauce as it oozed from his donut.

"I'm on the Protein Donut Diet. You can lose five pounds a week on it," Julian said.

"Five pounds is a lot," Tubman said, picking up the few remaining crumbs of his dessert with his fingers and licking them clean.

"That's average for the Donut Diet, Sir. I've lost a pound a day so far," Julian said.

"I thought it was your clothes making you look thinner."

Forest beamed. "I'll tell my wife. She loves donuts. It's because of Strawberry Puffs that she got so fat in the first place. She had morning tea at her tennis club every day and she ballooned right up."

"You could lose a few pounds yourself," Fry said under her breath.

"You ought to sue Dough Inc., Hank," Tubman suggested. "Intentional inflection of emotional distress."

"I think that's infliction, Sir," Julian said. "Everyone should go on the Donut Diet. You lose fat, and it's fun!"

187

"It works for kids too. We had 62 preteens in our latest study at Columbus Elementary. On average, they each lost four pounds in a week; 75 percent lost at least three pounds; and 25 percent lost five pounds or more. Here's the proof," Doctor Fry said, slapping a ten-page stapled report on the table.

"*An Evaluation of the Donut Diet at Columbus Elementary School*," Tubman read. He frowned. "Aren't they the same kids who sold drugs to their teachers."

"You're thinking of a school in Colombia, Sir," Julian whispered.

"*Columbus Calorie Counters*, Governor," Fry sighed.

"Right! Julian's *Kids Kounting Kalories*. I glad we changed the name before the campaign. Wasn't there a plump kid who started it? Her mother's a VP at Dough Inc. Talk about hypocrisy."

"Claire Bussomfeld lost eight pounds in the first week of our donut study, Governor. You should see the difference it's made to her self esteem."

"It took me a year to lose eight pounds! Frankly, I find it hard to believe."

"It's all in there," Fry said, pointing at her report. "The results speak for themselves. Governor, I request permission to switch the contract for the school lunch program to Healthy American Donuts."

"It's not just about kids losing weight, Francine," Tubman muttered. "There are other considerations."

"You're right about that. Teachers at Columbus Elementary reported vastly improved attention spans during the study, wide-awake kids who were eager to learn, and..."

"People are furious about the deficit," Tubman interrupted. "The word got out we're paying $5.89 for a diet school lunch.

Fry was flabbergasted. "That's highway robbery for a frozen taco and refried beans."

"We set up a prices commission to stop companies from taking advantage, didn't we Julian?"

"I expect the Excessive Prices Agency got confused, Sir. They changed the sizes of donuts at the same time as prices skyrocketed, and some companies changed hands. Plus we had the Thanksgiving holiday right in the middle."

"I'm sure two donuts per child will be cheaper, Governor," Fry said sarcastically.

"There are complications." Tubman stalled, glancing at Forest for support.

"Some people want salads for the veggie-kids. The next thing will be kosher diets for Jewish kids. Then, it'll be Muslim kids. God only knows what the Hindus and Buddhists will ask for."

"Then, offer alternatives," Fry said.

Tubman took over. "An Arugula salad costs $7.49 on the cafeteria tray! Do you have any idea what kosher costs, Doc?"

"My brother's partner is Jewish. I can ask him, if you want?"

Tubman gave a dismissive wave. "No need. I agree diet donuts are the way to go. Kids love them. However, we have to check out the factory, make sure it meets our standards, that sort of thing. Next year, after the election, when things aren't so pressured..."

"Governor, I'm doing an interview this afternoon with Jordan Ryder. I know he's going to ask about the school diet program. I'd like to include diet donuts."

Forest looked up. "Don't trust Ryder for a moment. He's with Media Services Network. They lie all the time."

"He sounds very nice on the telephone, Mr. Forest."

"And so do I, Francine," Tubman interjected. "The State can't sign contracts with just anyone. Who knows what they're putting into their donuts?"

"So ask for their recipes."

Chapter 31.

Jeffrey leaned out of the office window and bellowed, "Dad, phone call for you."

"I'll be right up," Jeremy shouted over his shoulder.

"Kids go fer sweet, Mr. McTavish," Dutch said, still seeking direction.

Dutch Hickman was in charge of mixing ingredients. He had no mixing expertise to speak of—his last job was loan examiner for a home-mortgage bank; before that, telemarketing stay-sharp knives; and before that, repairing used household appliances. He was panhandling at a freeway exit when Jeremy drove up. Dutch's sign 'will work for donuts' got him hired on the spot—he was Healthy American Donuts' first employee. His first pay check was $27.95 for one day, and as many donuts as he could carry out the door.

"Did you hear any more from Babcock?" Jeremy asked.

"He called again last night and offered me a thousand bucks to join his team, Mr. McTavish," Dutch replied. "I told him it wasn't about dough. He wouldn't take no for an answer. He kept on asking me questions?"

Jeremy flinched. He'd borrowed heavily to start the company, invested all of his life-savings, sold his house, and even traded his Triumph sports car for a minivan so old he had to wind down the windows for a breath of fresh air.

"What did he want this time? More recipes?"

"He wanted to know why our donuts cost so much. I told him it cost us 39 cents to make a donut. I didn't realize it was important. I'm sorry."

"It can't be helped. Just be careful from now on."

Yawning like a narcoleptic hippopotamus on a hot summer day, Jeremy scooped dough from the ladle and tasted. "Put in three pounds of raw sugar," he decided, already headed back to his office.

The Healthy American Donut Company factory was a testament to Scottish frugality. It was 74 years old, left over from when Detroit was king. Across the Midwest, a hundred plants had once churned out gigantic, gas-guzzling cars with ridiculous tail fins. The factory had a roof like a cheese grater, with north-facing skylights, and steel columns that looked like skinny aspen trees. Now, everything that wasn't painted snow-white, either sparkled like crystal wine glasses, or gleamed brighter than hospital equipment.

He stopped on the landing, catching his breath after the long flight of stairs from the factory floor. Below 100-series machines clashed, clanged, and clinked their way through 10,329 donuts each hour, still nowhere near full capacity.

"You look exhausted, Mr. McT."

Jeremy nodded tiredly. "Long day, Frodo."

"Jeff said you're home at midnight and you leave again at four."

Jeremy and Jeffrey called a recycled school bus home. It doubled as the company's marketing vehicle, spending the day at malls and trade shows. Pictures of over-sized donuts covered the outside, including most of the windows. Inside were racks for different types of donuts. There were also displays of donut memorabilia, like a mummified donut from King Tut's tomb, and a donut with a bite out of it, supposedly taken by Marie Antoinette on her way to the guillotine.

"I'm trying to get the next production line up and running," Jeremy explained.

The third production line was nearing completion, while the machines for the fourth line sat on recycled pallets.

"There' s a call for you," Frodo reminded him.

"You're getting taller," Jeremy said.

"An inch since summer camp. Every bit helps. Mom says it's your donuts." Frodo grinned constantly, even when he headed off to do homework.

Jeremy watched him bounce down the stairs, wondering where he found the energy. He went into the office, picking up a chocolate Vitamin Splurge on the way, 85 calories, 100-percent natural ingredients, FDA-approved, and guaranteed to ward off colds if eaten regularly.

"… esophagus, stomach, small intestine. He hung up, Dad. Big intestine, colon, rectum, ew, gross!" Jeff had his feet on the table, his biology book open at 'digestive tract.'

"Who hung up?"

"Didn't say. Mouth, esophagus, stomach…"

With a defeated shrug, Jeremy headed to the Donut Discovery Center, aka new product development; where he'd personally installed everything from his previous kitchen (except the kitchen sink) in the rear of the office and divided it off with gold lame curtains he'd found in a dumpster.

"What are you working on?" Jeff asked.

"What do Santa's elves eat for Christmas?"

Jeff thought for a moment. "A cranberry Elf Nut with green icing?"

"Not red and green."

"Nutmeg and cinnamon." He licked his lips as if tasting it. "And chocolate. It would be different inside, too, 'fruit cakey', and gooey."

"That would be your great grandmother's Christmas pudding when she didn't cook it long enough."

"We could wrap them in colored foil, with ribbons like presents," Jeff suggested.

"Brilliant, my boy! Get on the Internet and find foil in bulk."

Jeremy hummed as he worked; mixing small batches of dough, spices, sultanas, raisins, and currants, with glace cherries and figs. In every case, the result was too dry. No one really liked dry fruitcake except little old English spinsters, and then it was because they doused it with exotic liqueurs.

Almost asleep on his feet, whim as much as frustrated hunch caused him to put two cups of mixed fruit and a cup of No. 4 chocolate-tofu sauce in his new industrial-grade blender, turning it into a paste, most of which he injected into a spiced-up Elf Nut.

"Santa must be a gourmet!" Jeff exclaimed after his very first bite.

The phone rang again.

"We need a secretary," Jeremy yawned as he went to answer it.

"Mr. McTavish, my name is Julian Whitebread. I'm assistant to Governor Tubman. I'm calling you about your healthy donuts. They're very good by the way. I eat them all the time, and not just because I switched from the Virtual Diet to the Donut Diet."

"How may I help you?" Jeremy muttered before he yawned into the phone.

"Are you sitting down, Mr. McTavish?"

Jeremy squinted at the clock on the wall, either 5:50 pm or 11:29 pm.

"Mr. McTavish, the Governor wants to know if you're interested in being the primary provider for his School Diet initiative. He's very excited after seeing the numbers."

"What numbers?" Jeremy yawned and rested his forehead on the wall.

"I've got them here somewhere. Seventy-five percent lost three or more, 50 percent lost four, and 25 percent lost at least five."

"That's a lot of numbers." Another wide-open yawn didn't restore reason.

"Two sixth-grade classes at Columbus Elementary ate your donuts for morning snack for five days, Mr. McTavish. The grand total was… this is truly unbelievable… 245 pounds!"

"That's the same as I weigh."

"It's exciting, isn't it Mr. McTavish? Who would've thought donuts would put an end to obesity? You'll have to start right away if you get the contract."

"Start what right away?"

"Shipping, of course. We need them delivered next Monday; five hundred…"

"Five hundred is no problem at all."

"Thousand."

Jeremy's head jerked up. "How many?"

"Two donuts per child comes to 500,000 a day; that's just for the schools in this area, Mr. McTavish."

"That's a lot of donuts, Mr. Whitebread."

"If you get the contract, it's just the start. Doctor Fry also wants to offer your donuts on the state-funded diet plan; however, she needs the recipes so she can approve them. You can fax them to me."

"I'll do it right away."

"Ask him how much they'll pay per donut?" Jeffrey interrupted.

"My VP of Finance wants to know how much," Jeremy said, shaking out cobwebs. "Per donut."

"The lawyers will need to review your proposal, Mr. McTavish, state regulations and all that. I'm sure the price will be more than enough to cover your costs with a tidy profit."

"We need to know up front," Jeff said quietly. "Tell him our bulk rate is $1.00. No, $1.08."

"One dollar," Jeremy said. Jeff frowned and shook his head. "And eight cents. One dollar eight cents."

"I'll inform the Governor, Mr. McTavish."

"Tell him that's as low as we can go," Jeff whispered. "We're barely covering our costs."

"Healthy donuts are very expensive to make. That's the best we can do," Jeremy said. Jeffrey nodded vigorously.

"I understand. I'm glad you're joining the team, Mr. McTavish. There is one more matter. I shouldn't say this, conflict of interest and all that; however, the Governor's Healthy Choices initiative needs your support. It's win-win all around."

Jeremy agreed to make a campaign donation and put down the phone. "It's going to be a very long night."

Chapter 32.

"Healthy American Donut's taking over diet school lunches," Leo complained, hurrying into the Boardroom. "My wife just called me. It's all over the Internet."

"I've heard it's not just the diet lunches; it's all diets!" Regina said, entering right on his heels.

"All of them! ALL OF THEM?" Babcock bellowed.

"It's on the TV," Max Nussbaum said, looking up at the stock price monitor.

"'Panic selling of NUT shares at seven cents. Healthy Choices CEO Dr. Francine Fry tells reporter Healthy American Donut Company will supply next year's school lunches.'"

"We can all read, Leo!"

"Donut and coffee, Mr. Babcock?" Ms. Wick asked sweetly.

"I'm flabbergasted! I was counting on Cal's lunch contract for operating funds."

"This is ridiculous!" Leo said as the stock price bounced between 5 and 6 cents.

"Man the lifeboats! Abandon ship!" someone called from the office outside.

"I need suggestions," Babcock said, taking a firm grip of his cell-phone.

"SWOT, Mr. Babcock. That's what Mr. Stiche would do. He'd write our strengths on the white board."

"Ms. Wick, it would help if you focused on taking notes of the meeting."

"Kids like Cal Foods' tacos," Fingledorp said, looking around the Boardroom for someone who wasn't scowling.

"Definitely a strength," Babcock muttered. "Okay, give me some more strengths."

"Marketing; as in the i-Team," Renard added, also looking around for support.

"Other strengths?" The silence went on and on. "That's it, then. Cal's lousy tacos and the i-Team."

Regina raised her hand. "Maybe you're better off asking for suggestions, Tom."

"Suggestions, anyone?"

"Like I said before, we under-price them. When they run out of money, we buy them out," Renard said. "My professor at Harvard called it the tire and acquire strategy!"

"I call it dumb," Regina interrupted.

"There's no need to be rude."

Regina shoved back her chair. "Healthy donuts are a whole new market." She stalked across the room to the whiteboard. On the monitor, NUT seemed have stopped at five cents a share. "They could charge $5 a donut and still sell them! They might even sell more. People want their donuts! Not ours! We can't under-price them!"

"So I made a mistake. There's no need to get upset at me," Renard complained.

"If your i-Team was doing its job we'd have competing products in the stores by now," Regina fired back.

"Except we don't know the formula," Renard replied crossly.

"It's this easy!" She wrote 'Healthy = Vitamins + protein + low cal + anti-ox' on the whiteboard.

Renard was red in the face. "It takes time to invent something like that."

"How hard can it be? Four friggin' cents now," Babcock grumped, clutching his cell phone with white knuckles.

"The i-team's working on it, Tom. It's harder than you think to reverse-engineer donuts."

"I'm not asking you to copy them," Regina said, underlining 'healthy' three times.

"I'd settle for a good imitation," Leo countered.

"Our 500s are the best in the industry. We can produce at a third of their cost. All we need to do is get close to their donuts and we'll out-compete them," Max Nussbaum said brightly. He looked years younger with his hair dyed black.

"Pook said they've applied for patents," Regina said.

"It hasn't stopped us in the past. Cal Foods had three patents for Big Nuts," Leo remarked.

Regina turned on her only friend in the Boardroom. "They would've sued us if we hadn't bought them out."

"I'm not worried about lawsuits," Renard said, raising his voice. "They won't have any money left to hire a lawyer after a price war. That's my no-cash-no-hassles strategy."

"So get the i-Team working to copy their flaming donuts!" Babcock ordered.

"It'll still take time, Tom. I don't have any one left on staff who's trained for that sort of thing."

"What happened to them?"

"I fired them. You said to focus on global strategies, not product development."

"Steal the recipes if you have to," Babcock said, chilling most of the room.

Regina shook her head. "Mr. Stiche has his faults; however, he'd never say Dough should steal from another company."

Ms. Wick nodded in agreement until she caught Babcock's eye.

"Can't you tell when I'm joking?" Babcock said, trying to laugh.

"What Mr. Stiche would do is call the Governor," Leo said with a slow sly smirk.

Suddenly, Babcock cackled and flipped open his cell phone. He sold all of his 82,500,000 shares for four cents each before he called Herman Stiche.

Chapter 33.

"Governor Tubman's office. You're speaking to Julian Whitebread, his aide. "

"Who's that?" Governor Stanley B. Tubman demanded, polishing his golf ball with a soft lambskin chamois.

Julian clamped his hand over the front of his cell phone. "Herman Stiche, Sir."

"What's Dough Inc. want now?" Forest asked, practicing his swing. He always felt self-conscious when he teed off first.

"I'll ask him." Julian raised the phone to his ear. "The Governor's very busy at the moment. Can I help? Yes, I understand. I'm not sure what the Governor can do about donut sales. He really can't tell the Legislature what to do." He covered his cell phone again. "He demands to speak with you, Sir."

Tubman growled, yet took the phone. "Good afternoon, Herman. It's a pleasure... Yes, I remember. Quid pro quo? What quid and quo do you have in mind?"

He smirked at Forest.

Forest smiled back. "Two cats in the bag, Stan?" he whispered.

Tubman nodded. "The recipes? Actually, we already have them. Yes, all of them. I'm not sure that's appropriate. Perhaps we should meet privately?"

"What's the deal?" Forest whispered.

Tubman cupped his hand over the cell phone. "The idiot's going on about his yacht. Something about fishing for virgins with his friend, Marlin."

"He's in the US Virgin islands, Sir," Julian said. "Marlin fishing is big there."

"He wants the recipes," the Governor whispered.

"What's he offering?"

"A campaign donation of $1,000,000."

Forest pointed up.

"Not enough quid for the quo, I'm afraid, Herman.... That's closer. To save some time here, I was thinking of a number closer to ten... I am being serious." He cupped his hand over the phone again. "The tight wad won't go any higher than two million."

"Capitalist pigs are all the same," Forest chuckled. "Tell him five million and let him stew, Stan."

"Governor," Julian interrupted. "My professors said negotiating with the private sector is easier if you use percentages. They're used to talking rates of return."

Tubman nearly took out his frustration on his cell phone. "Herman, I'm sure we can work something out." He closed his eyes and considered which course to take. "I'll have my people call your people tomorrow. Actually, my people are much better at taking phone calls than making them. Have your people call my people."

Julian gave the Governor an ungrateful look. Being left out of the loop diminished his self-esteem.

"Better yet, go through Julian. He's my right hand."

Julian beamed as bright as the Caribbean sun.

"So what's Dough Inc. doing in the Virgins, Herman? You have Big Nuts there too? It's really tax deductible? You ought to try the healthy ones... They're good, aren't they? We had low-cal desserts at a State Dinner for the Chinese Free Trade Delegation. They loved 'em!"

Tubman closed the phone and handed it back to Julian. He rubbed his chin. "He'll pay. The only problem is how to set it up."

"We can't just hand McTavish's recipes to them," Forest said, thinking aloud.

"Actually, we can," Julian said, nodding eagerly. "We use eminent domain!"

"Eminent domain's for real estate," Forest sneered. "There's no point taking their factory."

"My professor said the State can take any property it wants if it's for the public good," Julian said.

"Your professor's an idiot."

"It's a sovereign right! It's in the U.S. Constitution, the Fifth Amendment, the Just Compensation clause."

"They put it in there to feed the frigging army!" Forest said. "I know the Constitution backwards, forwards, and sideways. I studied it in college for extra credit."

"It says 'nor shall private property be taken for public use, without just compensation'," Julian argued. Forest would've been red up to his ears. "That's means any private property is fair game!"

"Any real property!" Forest said, looking Julian straight in the eye.

"Any property! It doesn't have to be real! Clark versus Nash, 1902. It was over water rights. It just has to be for the public good!"

"Bush, 13406?" Tubman said, raising his hand for law and order.

203

"What?" Julian and Forest said together.

"Executive order signed June 23, 2006. Using eminent domain requires just compensation, purpose benefitting the general public, and..." Tubman paused for effect. "NO advancing the economic interest of private parties that are given ownership or use of the property."

"Ohhhh!" Julian groaned. "It was such a good idea too."

"Except it only applied to the Federal Government. It's 'open sesame' for us."

"You mean 'open season' don't you, Sir?"

"No I mean 'open sesame.' A veritable treasure awaits us. All we have to show is the public benefit of taking property."

"How does the public good include recipes for...?"

"People benefit by losing weight. Public good right there!" Tubman interrupted.

"The other route is we're breaking up a monopoly. It's obvious as the nose on Fry's face that McTavish is overcharging for his donuts," Forest remarked, repeating what his wife had said (not the part about Fry's nose—he made that up himself).

"Good point, Hank," Tubman muttered. "Dr. Fry's been after me to fix the price of a healthy donut at 50c each across the board. It's not healthy how much she worries about the less fortunate."

"McTavish is demanding $1.08 from the government for school lunches; that's definitely a monopoly in my book!" Forest said.

"McTavish is getting rich on government largesse, Governor. That's not right! Plus he can't make enough donuts to meet our needs; either that or he's deliberately restricting supply to keep prices high," Julian added.

"That sounds like an unfair business practice to me," Forest said gleefully.

"So we use eminent domain and share his recipes with other companies to make the market competitive again. The public good is being served when people lose weight," Tubman agreed with a smile. "The only question is compensation. How much do you think McTavish is making, Hank?"

Forest shrugged. "I figure close to a million bucks a day."

"You're joking!"

"He's got four lines making 60,000 donuts an hour, and he had to add an extra shift for the school donuts."

"No one should be making a million bucks a day," Tubman said angrily. "The compensation we'll have to pay him... it's mindboggling!"

"There might be a way," Julian mused.

Chapter 34.

Jeremy snoozed with his head on his desk. The buzzing was endless, even worse with his eyes closed. It felt like he had a sinus infection, pressure behind his temples, aching jaws, watering eyes. If he listened hard, he could hear the factory over the buzzing. Electric motors whirred, conveyor belts humming, warning bells at the end of cooking cycles, and an occasional loud bang as a forklift dropped raw ingredients into the hoppers.

He put the telephone back in its cradle and rolled his chair across to the window. His chair was an antique of the industrial age with wood arm rests, horse-hair padding in the seat, and brass wheels in the legs. Below, 61,026 donuts per hour streamed off four production lines and onto big metal trays, then onto the same conveyor that once carried finished car engines to the shipping area.

Nearly 2,000 Healthy American Donut employees busily sorted, stacked, loaded, emptied, cleaned, polished, repaired, and ate donut snacks. For most, if not all of them, it was the best job they'd ever had; a generous salary, health insurance, retirement at age 58, and profit sharing.

Jeremy reached for the button on the side of the wall. The emergency siren blasted into every corner of the sprawling factory, from the front office, to the storage rooms, vibrating through the main production area, all the way to the loading dock, and out to the recycling dumpster. With a groan, 87 100-series machines shut down in predetermined order, mixers, cookers, icers, injectors, even the glazing machines, which he'd converted to low-cal alternatives. Conveyors slowed to a crawl, and then stopped. People turned and stared up at the office window. Jeremy waved through the glass and slowly stood up.

"I've got an announcement to make," he said as he passed through the office.

Jeff, who was out of school for the holidays, knew something was wrong. He picked up the military-issue megaphone and a stool and followed a step or two behind his father. By the time they reached the landing, the employees were gathering below.

"How's the new car working out, Toby?" Jeremy called to one of the 34 maintenance staff. He got a wave back.

"When's the big day?" he called to Snoozie, really Patricia. With four kids under five she had a sleep problem. For an hour a day, she snoozed next to her injector-machine.

"The 24th, Mr. McTavish, Sir. We're calling him Jeremy if it's a boy."

Jeremy shouted, 'A bonnie name for a laddie' and gave a 'thumb's up.' He knew all but a few of his employees by name. The ones he didn't know had been hired in the last couple of days. It would take another trip or two around the factory before he remembered them.

He waited for the stragglers, bantering with employees. Finally, when the front of the factory was a sea of heads, Jeffrey handed him the megaphone. It screeched like an air raid siren when he switched it on.

"Happy New Year," someone shouted.

Jeremy blinked and tried hard to smile. "I've got something to say. It won't take long." He swallowed. "This is terrible timing. I was planning to give everyone two weeks' pay as an end-of-the-year bonus. I just got off the phone with Tom Babcock. For those who don't know, he's president of Dough Inc."

"He's a thievin' @$$hole!" Dutch shouted.

"The Governor has used his power of eminent domain to give Dough Inc. the recipes for all of our donuts," Jeremy said, looking over his factory. "It gets worse." He took a deep breath. "The law requires just compensation based on the market value of what's taken. That would be our donuts, most of which sell at over a buck; however, we've been accused of price gouging by the Excessive Prices Agency."

"No way! They're worth every cent."

"People don't have to buy them!"

"We sell 'em cheap!"

Jeremy nodded in agreement. "It doesn't matter. The Governor has fixed the price of our donuts at 40 cents, which is our cost plus a penny. The compensation isn't enough to cover what I borrowed to buy our equipment. We're out of business, effective immediately. I'm sorry, everyone. The end-of-year bonus is now severance pay."

There was a collective groan, "No!"

"What about the school lunch program, Mr. McTavish?"

"Dough's put in a bid to provide our healthy donuts at 38 cents each, a penny less than our cost. They'll still make a profit because they don't have our labor cost with their new equipment."

"It's not fair?" Toby yelled.

"Damn robots!"

"They'll force us out of business, and then raise their prices."

"Babcock ought to be in jail!"

"The Governor, too!" someone else shouted.

"Babcock and Tubman in a cell with Bubba! That's worth losing my job to see!"

"You got that right!" Jeremy shouted back before he realized he was still using the megaphone. "The thing is..." He sighed and slowly shook his head. "People can't compete with machines."

"We'll work for donuts, Mr. McTavish," Dutch yelled.

"Donuts or nothing!" someone shouted.

Then, from the back of the crowd, even louder...

"Donuts! Donuts! Donuts! DONUTS! DONUTS!!"

It went on and on until Jeremy switched off his loudhailer and then on again. The siren got their attention.

He waved to the crowd. "I appreciate the offer; however, it'll just prolong the agony."

"How did they get the recipes, Mr. McTavish?"

"Babcock said the government decided we were charging too much and gave them the recipes to increase competition."

"That'd be spread-the-wealth-around Tubman."

"More like a reward for donating to his campaign fund."

"It's not fair!"

Lanky Jeffrey McTavish stood up on the stool. "My dad's worked too hard to deserve this! We need to fight back! Let's march on the State House," he yelled, brandishing a stirring spoon.

"Sue the government!

"Take them to court, Mr. McTavish!"

"Donuts!"

"Donuts! Donuts!"

"DONUTS! DONUTS! DONUTS!"

Jeremy used the siren again. "I'm as upset as you are, but I'm not going to automate the factory just to make a profit. We don't have the money for a court battle. Even if we could sue the government, which we can't unless they agree to be sued, we'd probably lose. I'm sorry; I'm closing the factory after this shift ends."

Mouths dropped open. People stared. Heads shook. Jeffrey hopped from the stool, no longer the clumsy overweight kid that other kids avoided.

"There isn't a choice. I wish there was; there's not." Jeremy waved his arm. "We have a first class factory with 2,000 great people working in it; however, being successful in business takes more than that. When I was working at Dough, the owner, Herman Stiche, always talked about competitive advantage. Ours was our recipes for healthy donuts; and we lost it."

He stepped back from the railing and handed the loudspeaker to Jeffrey. He blinked like a ginger monkey with dust in his eyes.

"What now, Dad?"

"I'm thinking of teaching at chef school."

"What about our Santa donuts? We're supposed to start making them tomorrow."

Jeremy let out a long sigh. "We'll stay open another day, okay?"

"Dad, I know orange isn't festive, but Frodo and I think you should include some Passion fruit syrup in the filling."

Chapter 35.

"NUT's back at $1.15 y'all," Stiche announced with a grin. He'd grinned nonstop since he'd bought 65 percent of Dough Inc. at four cents a share.

He also grinned when he looked at his freshly painted portrait, placed at the front of the Stiche family line. He'd flown the artist in from Miami, sitting for hours while the artist dabbed paint on canvas. 'Inspiring,' he'd heard a few people say when they saw it, although several had turned up their nose. Instead of a Boardroom chair, the artist had painted him sitting in a fishing chair on the stern of *Marlin Mad*, with a large yellow fin tuna hanging behind him.

With a suntan, and a Chicago Bulls cap, he looked relaxed, yet determined. Ms. Wick particularly liked his Caribbean shirt, neon blue with yellow and pink conch shells all over it.

"It's good to have you back, Herman," Ms. Wick said, as much smitten by her employer's Caribbean aura as her new job as Executive Secretary.

"It's good to be back in the saddle..." For the life of him, he couldn't think of Ms. Wick's first name. "Could you pass me one of those Vitamin Splurges, please?"

"Vitamin Surge is what we're calling them," Babcock snapped, no longer sitting at the head of the table. He was squashed between a geriatric Max Nussbaum and a smirking Regina.

"I do miss my Strawberry Puffs," Stiche said, in abundant good humor. "Let's start with a sales report."

Renard opened his notebook. "Overall it's lots of good news, Sir. Total donut sales are up another three percent this month,

Mr. Stiche. Of course, those are all healthy donuts. Also, our X-Nuts have received quite a few complaints since last month."

"Only to be expected after we shifted from Passion fruit syrup to artificial flavors," Leo grouched.

"Our regular donut sales are down five percent, except for doggy donuts; those are down 21 percent," Renard continued, unruffled. "We're also getting lots of complaints about fat dogs."

"What are we doing about it?"

"The i-Team is looking into it, Mr. Stiche."

"Look into it faster."

"Yes, Mr. Stiche."

"How about a production report, Max? Max? Max! MAX!"

Max Nussbaum jerked awake. "What?"

"Production report, please."

"Everything's humming along, Herman. We're running at 82 percent capacity."

"Quality control?"

Leo had a PowerPoint presentation. "Quality control continues to be a problem," he summarized after ten minutes of means, standard deviations, and testing hypotheses. "Robots tend to miss small imperfections."

"Is it true one of our customers found a mouse in her Big Nut?" Stiche asked.

"Dead or alive?" Regina asked.

"I don't really know," Leo replied.

"It died when it was fried, Leo. Its tail was hanging out the side," Max Nussbaum chuckled.

"Not good enough, y'all!" Stiche exclaimed. His gaze settled on Tom Babcock. "What's our competitive advantage, Tom?"

"Great people making a quality product at a reasonable price... Mr. Stiche."

"What happens when people don't do their job, Tom?"

"You lose your competitive advantage, Mr. Stiche."

"That's right! Now, how about some suggestions on how to retain our competitive advantage, besides improving our quality control? Tom?"

Babcock tried an ambivalent shrug, squirming as everyone in the room stared at him. Even his chair was uncomfortable. It squeaked when he rocked back, and it didn't roll stealthily, not like his old chair.

Finally, Renard spoke again. "We need better products than our competitors, Mr. Stiche."

"That's correct, Sy. And how do we do that?"

"We do R&D, Mr. Stiche."

"Anything else?" Stiche asked.

Renard had to think. "We build the Dough brand."

"And we do that by focusing on..." Stiche prompted.

"Brand equity and customer service, Sir."

Leo added, "Herman, we shouldn't underestimate the importance of efficient production and distribution."

Ms. Wick put up her hand. "Employee relations, Mr. Stiche."

"And Public Relations," Regina added, inching sideways. She flipped open her dispenser. "Breath mint, Tom?"

"And you watch your competition like a hawk," Stiche added.

He looked around the room, thinking he might have the artist from Miami paint another portrait of him, better still, a portrait for each season, carefully posed like business proverbs. Winter could have an eagle behind him, watching his back, definitely symbolic. Fall would be Thanksgiving, and humble. Spring would be golf, and dedicated. His 'summer' portrait was inspiring, though an appropriate proverb eluded him. He smiled, remembering the moment.

"I caught that tuna on 60-pound line after a three hour struggle. It was almost a world record."

The tuna was 103 pounds short of a world record. Still, he'd had it preserved, taking pride of place on the wall of his office, iridescent scales accentuated with glossy varnish, an icon of man's love of nature.

"A remarkable achievement, catching a fish that big on 60-pound line," Leo enthused, hoping to make up for his mouse gaff.

"My point is…" Stiche took a breath. "It took persistence to land that fish. It's the same in business. Never giving up when the going gets tough. That's the Boy Scout motto for a reason."

"I always thought it was 'Be prepared,'" Nussbaum said.

"My father always said, 'When the going gets tough, the tough get going.' He was a Marine, so he'd know," Renard said.

"My father said 'don't give up when the going gets tough,'" Leo said. "That's the same as what Mr. Stiche just said."

"Herman, another Vitamin Surge, Splurge, whatever it's called?" Ms. Wick asked, already putting one on his plate with a fancy lace doily.

"What's McTavish doing, Babcock?"

"They're not making healthy donuts any longer, Mr. Stiche. Just those gooey fruit cakey things they brought out for the holidays."

"They're good," Max Nussbaum whispered to Ms. Wick.

"Petunia and I split a Fruity Frenzy for dessert every night. We do it like clockwork. It's always good," she whispered back.

THE END

About the Author

Neil Barry lives somewhere in the U.S., where he endeavors to keep a low profile in the Age of Surveillance. Born somewhere outside the U.S. many years ago, he attended graduate school at a nameless university on the East Coast, where he studied a subject completely unrelated to anything in this book. Later, he immigrated legally to the U.S., travelled extensively, raised an anonymous family, and built a less-than-stellar career as an academic at another nameless university in the Midwest. After 30 years of frustration, he escaped to retirement, and began writing books, including an acclaimed trilogy that can be discovered by searching for Neil Barry on the website of the #1 Internet retailer.

Despite rumors to the contrary, Neil Barry has not contributed to political campaigns, run for public office, made a Youtube video about how to tar and feather your US Congressman/ Congresswoman/Senator for ruining the country, or invented ways to make low-calorie donuts.

Neil Barry in snow storm, 2016. Copyright, Author